WOMEN AND
THE COMMON LIFE

WOMEN AND
THE COMMON LIFE

Love, Marriage, and Feminism

Christopher Lasch

edited by
Elisabeth Lasch-Quinn

W. W. Norton & Company
New York   London

The text of this book is composed in 11/14 Berling Roman
with the display set in Univers Black Extended
Composition and manufacturing by The Maple-Vail Book Manufacturing Group
Book design by BTD / Mary A. Wirth

LIBRARY OF CONGRESS CATALOGING-IN-PUBLICATION DATA
Lasch, Christopher.
Women and the common life : love, marriage, and feminism /
Christopher Lasch ; edited by Elisabeth Lasch-Quinn.
p.   cm.
Includes index.
ISBN 0-393-04018-6
1. Women—History.   2. Marriage—History.   3. Family—History.
4. Sex role—History.   5. Feminism—History.   I. Lasch-Quinn.
Elisabeth.   II. Title.
HQ1121.L37   1997
305.4'09—dc20   96-15988
                                                          CIP

W. W. Norton & Company, Inc., 500 Fifth Avenue, New York. N.Y. 10110
http://web.wwnorton.com
W. W. Norton & Company Ltd., 10 Coptic Street, London WC1A 1PU
1   2   3   4   5   6   7   8   9   0

CREDITS: "The Comedy of Love and the *Querelle des Femmes:* Aristocratic Satire
on Marriage" from *Mythmaking Frame of Mind: Social Imagination and American
Culture,* James Gilbert et al., eds. (Belmont, CA: Wadsworth, 1993), pp. 303–25.
Copyright © 1993. Reprinted by permission of Wadsworth Publishing Company.
"The Suppression of Clandestine Marriage in England: The Marriage Act of 1753"
from *Salmagundi,* 26 (Spring 1974). Reprinted by permission. "Gilligan's Island"
from *New Republic* (December 7, 1992). "The Mismeasure of Man" from *New
Republic* (April 19, 1993). Reprinted by permission. "Misreading the Facts about
Families" from *Commonweal* (February 22, 1991). Copyright © Commonweal
Foundation, 1991. Reprinted with permission of the Commonweal Foundation.
"The Mysteries of Attraction" from *Commonweal* (February 26, 1993). Copyright ©
Commonweal Foundation, 1993. Reprinted with permission of the Commonweal
Foundation. "The Sexual Division of Labor, the Decline of Civic Culture, and the
Rise of the Suburbs" from *The Meaning of the Family in a Free Society,* W. Lawson
Taitte, ed. (Dallas: The University of Texas at Dallas, 1991). From an address given
in the Andrew R. Cecil Lectures on Moral Values in a Free Society at The University
of Texas at Dallas. Reprinted by permission. "Life in the Therapeutic State" from
The New York Review of Books (June 12, 1980). Reprinted with permission from *The
New York Review of Books.* Copyright © 1980 Nyrev, Inc. "Bourgeois Domesticity,
the Revolt against Patriarchy, and the Attack on Fashion" began as one of the Freud
Memorial Lectures delivered at University College, London, in 1981.

Contents

v

Acknowledgments

The publication of this book would have been impossible without those who encouraged and assisted my father as he persevered on this project at the end of his life and who encouraged and assisted me after his death. Jean Bethke Elshtain's enthusiasm was vital in advancing the work. Nell Commager Lasch and Ray Lasch-Quinn helped immeasurably; their practical assistance and moral support for the particularly complex demands of this project sustained it at every stage. In the work's latter stages Rochelle Gurstein, Richard Wightman Fox, William Leach, and Robert West-

brook also read a draft of the introduction and their sugges-
tions and heartening responses further inspired the project.
Amy Cherry, the book's editor at Norton, contributed valu-
able assistance.

Though my father did not let me know his wishes for a
dedication, this collection makes it clear just how much he
treasured the quality of the life created by his "kindred spirits": friends, students, readers, fellow writers and teachers,
family members, and others. Their lively spirit and capacity
for commitments of all kinds prove that the common life
can, when nourished so well, not just exist but thrive.

We put our love where we have put our labor.
—RALPH WALDO EMERSON *Journals, 1836*

Introduction

In 1985 Christopher Lasch, my father, mentioned to me that he was reading Rousseau and Poullain de la Barre. When I asked him why, he wrote in a letter:

> Sometimes I ask myself the same question. I'm trying to trace the interconnections between the modern ideology of intimacy, the new domestic ideal of the nineteenth century, and feminism—something like that. It's called, tentatively, *The Domestication of Eros*. I've been working on it for a long time—about twenty-five years—but the focus

keeps changing. . . . Sometimes I wonder how I got myself into this tangle [March 12, 1985].

This collection of essays does not pretend to hold the resolution of Christopher Lasch's thinking on this imposing theme. In fact, in one of the most recent essays assembled here he refers to his "many years of inconclusive struggle with the subject." *Women and the Common Life*, however, offers some of his most absorbing forays into terrain that is both intriguing and confounding in its complexity. Taken together, these essays suggest a number of reasons why Christopher Lasch, historian and social critic, might have gotten himself "into this tangle."

Writing about women well before the field of women's history came into its own in the 1970s and 1980s,[1] Lasch was one of the very few historians who studied the roles that women, feminism, love, marriage, and the family played in the history of the West, not only out of a passionate interest in these subjects but also out of a conviction that cultural history could not be understood otherwise. Rather than view women's history as a sideline to the rest of history, a specialization, or compensation for earlier studies that ignored or underrated the importance of women, he saw the history of women as inseparable from cultural history as a whole. In one essay included here, "The Mismeasure of Man," Lasch refers to Havelock Ellis's response to V. F. Calverton's proposed history of women: "The history of women could not be detached from the history of the human race in general, Ellis said, without reducing it to something 'slight & superficial & secondhand.' A serious history of women would become a history of intimacy—'a history of mankind in a more intimate sense than anything yet attempted.'" It is in fact the connections between the history of women and the

history of the West more generally that give these essays their coherence and significance.

In 1993 and 1994, while battling cancer, Christopher Lasch was at work on this collection of essays, deciding which previously published essays to include and revising "Bourgeois Domesticity . . . ," the only essay that has not been published elsewhere. At the same time he was finishing the work on his last book, *The Revolt of the Elites and the Betrayal of Democracy* (1995). Remarkably, he worked up to the very end of his life—through nausea, fatigue, and pain—completing *The Revolt of the Elites* ten days before he died on Valentine's Day 1994.

I was fortunate to be able to spend much time with my father in the last months of his life, becoming increasingly involved in the final stages of *The Revolt of the Elites* and this collection. The essays published here include only the pieces my father told me definitively that he wanted included; I followed his wishes exactly, at the risk of leaving out other essays of his that could easily and naturally have fit. The essays he decided to incorporate, I believe, complement one another beautifully, despite their coverage of a great range of subjects over a large span of time. I hope, as he would have, that interested readers will seek out the numerous other essays and articles he produced on related subjects, as well as his books, which elaborate his interpretations further, especially his full-length study of the family, *Haven in a Heartless World: The Family Besieged* (1977).

My aim has been to remain as true to my father's vision of this collection as possible. The previously published essays have been only lightly edited, mainly for typographical errors. "Bourgeois Domesticity . . . ," still unfinished at my father's death, required a title and a conclusion,[2] as well as a couple of transitional phrases, but is otherwise his own. The title of the collection, which we referred to simply as the "women essays" when it was in progress, suggested itself to me directly from the essays; I hoped it would capture the central themes without imposing an interpretation that was foreign to the work. Indeed, this brief introduction aims merely to point to some of the connective tissue that the essays themselves intrinsically possess.

The coherence of these essays is best expressed in that precise phrase from my father's letter to me ten years ago. While ranging from a discussion of the *querelle des femmes* of the Middle Ages to the "postmodern" family of the late twentieth century, the essays, as assembled, do make important "interconnections between the modern ideology of intimacy, the new domestic ideal of the nineteenth century, and feminism." While there are sometimes frustrating contradictions in the essays[3]—explained by developments in his thinking, in some cases, and unresolved questions, in others—several themes emerge: changing marital ideas and practices; feminism's link to the history of the middle class and the family; a counter-tradition of love; the history of self-respect; and the rationalization of everyday life. In many ways it is this rationalization of life that provides an overarching explanation for the changes in conceptions of love, marriage, and feminism analyzed in these short works.

Much of modern life, in Lasch's portrait, rests on the assumption that all realms of activity should come under intense scrutiny, that science and rationality can best lead to an understanding of human experience, and that only trained experts can direct the conduct of daily existence. The reordering of life according to such principles of rationalization resulted from the tendency of corporate capitalism and the modern liberal state to expand their power, which they accomplished by means of a bureaucratic structure and paternalistic ethos. The service professions, acting on behalf of the state, intruded into the private domain, helping to replace habit and custom with esoteric techniques for addressing everyday problems, causing a situation of dependence on elites that is antithetical to democracy.

The subjection of all of life to scrutiny, surveillance, and ultimately manipulation by outside experts led to a degradation of the common life, a rich dimension of human experience and, to Lasch, both a prerequisite for and a goal of democratic citizenship. Characterized by competition and cooperation with others toward a shared end, the common life (often an extension of family life) springs from voluntary gatherings in which the lines of work, play, community organizing, socializing, and other purposes tend to cross. Fostering spontaneity, invention, and self-reliance, this arena transcends purely intimate contacts but steers clear of any source of external power, turning instead to its own set of rules and standards of fairness, excellence, and common sense, forged from experience and tradition. The common life not only nurtures the individual responsibility and courage demanded for democracy but provides the kind of life that is worth living in the first place.

The encroachment of professional expertise, and its reduction of human interaction into its component parts for the purpose of analysis, also have drastic results in the realm of intimacy. It is no wonder, Lasch shows us, that modern life seems "too highly organized, too self-conscious, too predictable." Reliance on purely scientific ways of understanding humanity and ordering experience results in a reductionist view of human nature "unadorned" by artistic and literary insight. The role of mystery, play, passion, and other qualities

cannot be easily managed. Lasch believes that the rationalization of life has in fact caused a "drastic shrinkage of our imaginative and emotional horizon."

It is this shrinkage—of the common life, of intimacy, of
our imaginations—that gives unity to the following works of
scholarship. Lasch calls on us to place the history of women
in the context of this cultural transformation and, in doing
so, to see the historical constraints on feminism, the family,
and love.

In Part One Lasch's first four essays allow us to envision a
world before and during this process of rationalization, as
they situate particular strains of thought about women in
their historical context. Rather than one long story of unre-
lieved patriarchal oppression, cultural history instead uncov-
ers a complicated mélange of customs and codes, some of
which were clearly superior to those that supplanted them.
In "The Comedy of Love and the *Querelle des Femmes*," Lasch
approaches the quarrel over women in medieval courtly life
less as a tradition of pure misogyny than as a lively, humorous
debate in which both men and women became objects of
satire. This debate climaxed around 1275 to 1280, when the
second part of *Roman de la Rose* was written by Jean de
Meun. Rather than view de Meun's work as an evil-spirited
diatribe against womankind and, in turn, the poem's critics
(like Christine de Pisan) as "protofeminists"—the way Joan
Kelly, for instance, has depicted them—Lasch saw the *Roman*
as inspired by the contemporary obsession with marriage, the
revival of the art of disputation, and the cult of the comedy
of love. Above all, he viewed the *Roman* as "a kind of symposium on love." Both the *Roman* and its critics can only be
understood as sharing a world view in which marriage and

romantic love were considered mutually exclusive and men and women deemed destined to separate sexual roles: "Those who debated the pros and cons of womanhood did not concern themselves with the abstract question of whether nature makes one sex superior to the other. . . . The issue that presented itself to those times was not whether woman is equal to man in the abstract but rather in what social relationships is she his equal, in what relations his subordinate?" It was the Cartesian separation of mind and body and the Enlightenment belief that institutions can be altered by reason that paved the way for a questioning of inherent sexual roles and a new view of marriage.

The dominant interpretation of the long-term history of the family in Europe and America is that the dynastic view of marriage—in which romantic love and marriage were considered incompatible—gave way, by the nineteenth century, to the glorification of self-selected companionship based on romantic love. "The Mysteries of Attraction," a review of Jean H. Hagstrum's *Esteem Enlivened by Desire: The Couple from Homer to Shakespeare*, however, endorses Hagstrum's argument that a countertradition of romantic love existed long before the rise of the middle class in the West (usually considered the harbinger of modern marriage)—as far back as the ancient Greeks. Existing alongside a view of marriage as inherently unequal and of women's sexuality as dangerous, this countertradition held that marriage in its ideal form could combine sexual desire and mutual respect. Rather than act as a disruptive force, passion could civilize and democratize social relations. Though it was a minority experience, romantic love tempered patriarchal social arrangements; this "erotic ideal," as Hagstrum calls it, necessitated a view of woman as man's counterpart and a view of sexuality as something other than sinful or threatening. Lasch argues that the twentieth century in fact has seen a "revulsion against romantic love," a loss of a sense that passionate love and marriage can coexist, and a return to the fear of Eros as a dangerous force. Our time resorts to friendship as a safer, less demanding option than lifelong unions based on passionate attractions; a pared-down, factual understanding has replaced an "adorned" rendering of sexuality. Unlike its scientific version, artistic and literary depictions of sexuality often acknowledge the roles of mystery and impulse as appropriate foundations of a happy and durable marriage.

In "The Suppression of Clandestine Marriage in England: The Marriage Act of 1753," we find a specific case in which this erotic ideal surfaced, the case of clandestine marriage. Middle-class reformers and moralists, influenced by Protestantism and humanism, launched an attack on the custom validated in common law of "precontracts," by which engagements to marry, often accompanied by sexual intercourse, were considered as binding as marriage itself. The attack on such contracts eventually broadened to all marriages lacking parental approval, such as those "Fleet marriages" performed secretly by complicitous clergymen. This opposition to "clandestine marriages" culminated in the passage of the Marriage Act of 1753, which required the publication of banns and outlawed the enforcement of precontracts by ecclesiastical courts. The idea that sound agreements to stay together for life could be forged in the heat of sexual passion struck advocates of the Marriage Act as imprudent and even dangerous. The decision to marry, they believed, should be a mature, careful one, based on compatibility and not on physical attraction. Opponents of the law, however, gave voice to the older tradition that validated passionate love as the basis for lifelong union. Part of a larger drive "to discipline the lower classes," the modern marital ideal, then, not only condemned arranged marriage, as is often thought, but discouraged couples from completely following their own instincts.

The next essay, "Bourgeois Domesticity, the Revolt against Patriarchy, and the Attack on Fashion," forges a link between the modern ideal of intimacy, as represented by the Marriage Act, and feminism. Often depicted as a reaction against the egalitarian fervor of the eighteenth century, the glorification of a feminine domestic sphere (which scholars call the cult of domesticity) constituted, Lasch illustrates, part of a larger critique of the American and British middle class's eagerness to adopt aristocratic behavior. Both feminists, like Mary Wollstonecraft, and their critics, like Hannah More, opposed attempts to mold women, through fashionable education, into creatures of leisure and ornaments of status. Wollstonecraft opposed aristocratic codes of womanhood and love for making women either "slaves or tyrants" and favored a notion of middle-class marriage as a source of true friendship and equality. Hannah More likewise objected to the uselessness and frivolity of the aristocratic ideal for women, but she also opposed feminists for seeking to eradicate the differences between men and women. While late-eighteenth- and early-nineteenth-century feminists stressed the natural rights of women as a basis for social equality, in the mid-nineteenth century Elizabeth Cady Stanton and other feminists began arguing, for the sake of expediency, that women and men had fundamental intellectual differences. Ironically, those who believed in the cult of domesticity—seen as reactionary by many historians—added to the feminist critique of fashion to create a liberating notion of femininity. Women, as a result, were considered vital guardians of the moral order; maternal influence became a remedy for problems both in and out of the home.

While Kathryn Kish Sklar, Barbara Epstein, and others

have described this expansive notion of maternal influence as an avenue for women's fuller participation in nineteenth-century social reform, Lasch's essay finds the roots of that participation in the strange blend of feminism and antifeminism in the attack on aristocratic fashion. Further, it reveals that the promise inherent in the critique of upper-class sensibilities evaporated in the new forms of social and economic inequality brought by the nineteenth century. The specific context out of which the cult of domesticity emerged was characterized by the convergence of a critique of the aristocratic lady (and thus American slavery) and a new middle-class ideal of marriage based on mutual respect. The nineteenth-century domestic ideal did not re-create patriarchal relations but instead, Lasch contends, helped foster a new paternalism that had equally disastrous consequences for women. Many women embraced the cult of domesticity as an assertion of their authority. In the process they often treated doctors and others dispensing advice on domestic matters as allies. Ironically, their receptiveness to the ministrations of so-called experts paved the way for the hegemony of professionals and the therapeutic mentality and for the loss of women's own authority.

A clear image of this new form of elite control and its connections with the history of women emerges in Part Two. These five essays bring us into the modern period with an analysis of the relations among the modern family, the changing nature of work, feminism, and the cultural apparatus of the liberal state.

In "The Sexual Division of Labor, the Decline of Civic Culture, and the Rise of the Suburbs," Lasch further questions the truism that the cult of domesticity was somehow responsible for all further sexual inequality by associating femininity with domesticity. He pierces through the "undifferentiated image of the old days" as a time in which women were confined to the home by citing women's unparalleled civic activity, usually voluntary, as evidence that they actually had an important tradition of purposeful work outside the home. Women's contributions, he goes so far as to say, made the modern city "livable": The city's resources in "the great age of urbanism" derived from "the unpaid labor of women, who raised the money, performed the daily drudgery, and furnished much of the moral vision behind the civic renewal of the early twentieth century." The high level of voluntarism of course rested on domestic service, but also on strong neighborhoods, held together by a network of trust based on unpaid services exchanged among friends, relatives, and neighbors—a kind of barter system.

The middle class's move to the suburbs, which Lasch sees as a search for privacy or "freedom from obligations," dismantled this "informal system of self-help." Suburban life brought with it a deterioration of life for both men and women, as illustrated in Betty Friedan's *Feminine Mystique* and Paul Goodman's *Growing Up Absurd*, which Lasch juxtaposes as comparable treatments of the question of "how to revive a sense of vocation in a society destitute of any common purpose." The move to the suburbs hastened the loss of any sense of a higher culture: objective truths; common beliefs; shared ideals; sources of pride; purposeful work. Lasch points to the decline of their civic role as a major factor in the frustration women expressed by the 1960s. The new wave of feminism, he believes, was a direct response to "the suburbanization of the American soul." Later feminists focused on the division of labor between men and women as part of a universal patriarchal exploitation of women. Advocating careers for women in paid labor outside the home, they ignored the larger degradation of work and the decline of civic culture that underlay the new separation of spheres. Lasch's own vision of women's equality is tied to his vision of a common life that gives such equality its meaning and worth.

Lasch's strict adherence to an ideal of women's equality rooted in a common life in which women and men are judged according to the same standards is the centerpiece of "Gilligan's Island." Lasch returns to the question of essential differences between men and women in this discussion of Carol Gilligan's research on women in the late twentieth century, as presented in *In a Different Voice* and a book she cowrote with Lyn Mikel Brown, *Meeting at the Crossroads: Women's Psychology and Girls' Development*. Gilligan concludes from her psychological studies that men and women have essentially different selves; men define themselves in separation while women define themselves in relation to other people. She attacks the idea that the height of ethical development is the "masculine" model of dedication to abstract principle instead of the "feminine" nurturance of personal relationships. Lasch considers the notion of women's nurturing nature insidious; it is a "cliché" that leads to "habits of self-effacement and submission in women" and makes them "reluctant to claim their rights." The myth of feminine nurturance also perpetuates a double standard for women and men of "competence, performance, and moral development." Yet Gilligan believes that women should demand their rights, place self-development above self-sacrifice, and consider self-assertion virtuous rather than selfish, seemingly contradicting the feminine ethic of caring.

Lasch proposes instead an alternative to both egoism and altruism, neither of which is inherently rewarding or helpful to society. This alternative is what he calls the secret of those who are "blissfully self-forgetful": They derive self-respect and achieve "selflessness" from losing themselves in work or dedicating themselves to a tremendous challenge. Instead of a therapeutic notion of self-esteem, arrived at by changing the rules to make everyone winners, he advocates the mastering of "arduous, risky pursuits," the attempt to meet "impersonal standards," and the struggle toward an "ideal of perfection" as avenues toward genuine self-respect and respect from others.

"The Mismeasure of Man" shows that the decline of self-respect among men has as intricate a history as among women. This essay assesses the shift from women's history to the "social construction of gender," as exemplified by the rise of works in "men's studies" such as the recent books by Kevin White and E. Anthony Rotundo. Lasch asserts that confusion over gender is a characteristic of our own age and cannot necessarily explain historical movements in the past. The idea that the cult of the strenuous life among men in the late nineteenth century resulted from perceived threats to their masculinity, exacerbated by the rise of feminism, sidesteps the more important change represented by the decline of "informal associations devoted to collective self-culture," such as lectures, debating societies, and other aspects of "boy culture." The loss of play for its own sake and the supervision of children's recreations by adults were part of a larger "attempt to apply to everyday life the same administrative techniques that had been applied so successfully to the market and the state." The rationalization of daily life, carried out by the "new sciences and pseudo-sciences—home economics, sexology, social work, psychoanalysis, child development, the 'science' of pedagogy—," caused "a subjection to routines that drained the joy out of work and play and wrapped everything in a smothering self-consciousness." It is this rationalization, which affected women as well, that helps explain, in Lasch's mind, the ideal of the strenuous life, the search for the primitive, and later the "reassertion of heroism" or "return to the wild man" in writings such as those by Robert Bly. The administration, organization, and rationalization of life cause people to long for adventure and real challenges; in the absence of demands on their character, they lose hope, purpose, and self-respect.

In "Misreading the Facts about Families," a review of Judith Stacey's *Brave New Families*, Lasch pursues the idea that the essence of strength, equality, and self-respect—for any of us—derives from taking charge of our own lives, managing to maintain long-term commitments, and facing challenges head-on. When Stacey finds this sort of self-respect among certain working-class women, even those struck by numerous financial problems and other woes, she assumes that this is a manifestation of feminism, rather than a particular way of responding to experience. She interprets the ties that working-class women make with extended family members in order to survive financially as indications that they are pioneers of the "postmodern family." To Lasch, this is too rosy a reading of the tragic tales of downward mobility and disarray on which Stacey bases her evidence. Here, too, he questions the assumption that it was industrialism that confined women in limited and subservient roles in the nuclear family and doubts that the growing number of women in the workforce and the reliance of working-class women on informal networks of support represents, above all, a feminist advance rather than a response to grim economic realities.

In the final essay, "Life in the Therapeutic State," many of these themes reach a climax as Lasch returns to his critique of schools of thought on the modern family. He questions both the idea that the modern family, a bastion of egalitarianism and affection, represents unmitigated progress and the feminist view of the modern family as a new form of patriarchal oppression. In his discussion of the work of Carl Degler, Michel Foucault, and Jacques Donzelot, Lasch reinforces his point that women were not the victims of the cult of domesticity but had a hand in restructuring the family along its lines. To reformers, the family stood apart from the rest of social life as a necessary refuge from the brutal conditions of the marketplace. Because of its unique importance, they asserted, the family demanded constant attention from women and others specially qualified to oversee it. Many women embraced the new ethos, viewing its place for them as moral leaders of the family as a way of gaining power over family affairs. Women's alliances with doctors and other advisers had the unintended result of opening the women's homes to intrusion from outsiders and diminishing their own authority. The growing isolation and insularity of the family contributed to women's reliance on an army of experts.

Paradoxically, in Lasch's interpretation the trend toward privatization of the family was accompanied by the complete invasion of the family, which allowed for the triumph of a therapeutic ethos that buttresses the liberal nation-state. Privatization of the family, necessary for individualism, places "excessive emotional demands" on the relations among family members. The therapeutic apparatus steps in to smooth over these tensions. Shoring up its own power through surveillance and infiltration rather than outright force, the liberal state benefits from this crisis of the family. This "noncoercive, nonauthoritative, manipulative control" originally sought to undermine patriarchal control but created a new state authority, partly by undermining people's faith in the efficacy of their own actions. The intrusion of outside experts, the assumption of responsibility for individual and family life by professionals, and the larger rationalization of life leave people without the will and self-respect that come from being responsible for their own lives and from making a respected contribution to a higher purpose, one transcending self-interest.

These essays cross the usual boundaries between family history, women's history, and cultural history. They paint a picture of the broad shift in the West toward the rationalization of daily life and the loss of a common life beyond both personal and political realms, which became increasingly indistinguishable. Lasch rejects the theory of ageless male oppression and female victimization and shows how women had a hand in this momentous development. In fact, their revolution against patriarchal hierarchy was hijacked by new economic and social elites. Many women's embrace of the cult of domesticity and alliance with physicians helped them temporarily strengthen their position in the family but ended up giving outsiders even new powers. Later suffragists' adherence to progressives' "boundless faith in disinterested scientific expertise" and reformers' drive to control sexuality can be understood as part of a larger effort to subject all human activity to scientific observation and control.

The larger picture, then, is one in which the older traditions of patriarchy are traded for a new hegemony of the liberal state. Neither is desirable, in Lasch's view, but what is clearly his ideal is a life in which science does not constitute our sole way of understanding the world; there is no "colonization of the lifeworld" (as Habermas put it); the family is not patriarchal, overly privatized, or invaded by experts. Instead it is outward-looking, encompassing more than just the emotional needs of its members, creating a basis for a common life that is neither personal nor political, but the rich union of custom and spontaneity that forms the fabric of human life in the collective—the basis for any meaningful conception of equality or democracy.

A little over a week before he died, my father completed work on *The Revolt of the Elites*. In the months and weeks before that, I had the profound experience of being one of those to assist him on his last projects. I will never forget working side by side with him in the living room, which had become a working study, with a computer on the coffee table and papers everywhere, the room overheated to keep him warm. I joked to my husband that my father was keeping a "sweatshop." In a sense this was not far from the truth because increasingly we worked every possible hour of the day, my father making an adjusted routine according to each stage of his illness. The sweatshop's compulsion, though, was absent. Instead there was the strangest exhilaration. This was confusing; we seemed to be so content, even joyful at times, yet my father was dying.

Somehow, between frightening medical emergencies and worries, my parents created a space of peace and calm. That living room became, for me, a haven—not from a heartless world, though at times from a world that seemed to consider death separate from life. Sometimes it seemed almost sacred, with the slowed pace, the gentle voices of visitors, music playing, the reading aloud of a letter from a dear friend, someone napping, the seriousness and weight of what we had to face. At other times it was like a newsroom, with the adrenaline of what seemed like the most natural activity: working toward another deadline. The inner peace, and confrontation with death, seemed inextricably tied to the activity, visits with friends, and the outer world. At points the overarching reality of the limited time we had together seemed overcome by what was then, and still is, the time-lessness of the period during which my father faced death by choosing not only to live but to live a certain kind of life.

That my father chose to work until the very end, to carry on the normal activities of life despite such tremendous obstacles, is a measure of his commitment to the transcendent project of cultural activity that neither starts at our birth nor ends at our death. Even further, his choice is a measure of his belief that meaningful work is inseparable from life itself; when the two become entwined, they can produce deep satisfactions, joy, even fun. This book is one of the results of that choice.

On the day he finished *The Revolt of the Elites*, clearly tapping his remaining energy to do so, my father walked me to the door to see me off. Several days later I was to return, to spend his last days with my parents as he died. But that day our plan was that I would mail the manuscript to the publisher on the way to my flight back to New Haven, where I was on leave. As I held the manuscript, we embraced. Referring to our work together, he said, "We had fun, didn't we?"

We did. For the first time I fully understood what he must have grasped so many times before, just how liberating and exciting it is to lose oneself completely in the task at hand and to dedicate all one's energies to work that one considers so important that it is worth doing even—especially—in the face of death. Perhaps this is what he calls being "blissfully self-forgetful."

ELISABETH LASCH-QUINN
Syracuse University

NOTES

1. See, for instance, Christopher Lasch and William R. Taylor, "Two 'Kindred Spirits': Sorority and Family in New England, 1839–1846," *New England Quarterly* 36 (March 1963): 23–41, included in Lasch, *The World of Nations* (New York: Alfred A. Knopf, 1973); "Introduction" and editorial commentary in Lasch, ed., *The Social Thought of Jane Addams* (Indianapolis: Bobbs-Merrill, 1965); "Jane Addams: *The College Woman and the Family Claim*," "Woman as Alien," and "Mabel Dodge Luhan: *Sex as Politics*" in *The New Radicalism in America, 1889–1963: The Intellectual as a Social Type* (New York: Knopf, 1965); "Emancipated Women," *New York Review of Books* (July 13, 1967): 28–32; "The Woman Reformer's Rebuke" in *The World of Nations*.

2. He left a brief, unfinished sketch for the essay's conclusion. I retained nearly all of his original language but interspersed sentences of my own in order to connect the ideas from his sketch to the ones he developed in the body of the essay.

3. It would have been interesting to see how he would have placed the compelling argument in "The Sexual Division of Labor, the Decline of Civic Culture, and the Rise of the Suburbs" that suburbanization was what cut off families from informal social networks into his view of the larger trend toward the privatization of the family, which he traces to the nineteenth century in "The Therapeutic State." A clarification about friendship would also have been welcome; it appears as a retreat from lifelong affectionate commitments in "The Mysteries of Attraction" and, within marriage, as a retreat from passion in "The Suppression of Clandestine Marriage in England: The Marriage Act of 1753," but the basis for a rewarding, egalitarian marriage in "Bourgeois Domesticity, the Revolt against Patriarchy, and the Attack on Fashion." These and other apparent contradictions, however, only fuel the suggestiveness of the topics and interpretations Lasch offers by inviting and inspiring further inquiry.

PART ONE

Manners and Morals

1

The Comedy of Love and the Querelle des Femmes: *Aristocratic Satire on Marriage*

Feminism and the controversy about feminism are "eternal," we are told; they rise and fall in cycles "with the rise and fall of civilization and with fluctuations in public morality," wearing "masks so varied that it is necessary to look closely in order to recognize beneath them the same face." These words appear in the introduction to a study of French feminism, so called, in the time of Molière. Another of the older studies of early modern "feminism" opens with the same kind of assertion: "the quarrel of the sexes is eternal." Still another announces, in the very first paragraph: "In all times, and in

almost all countries, there has been a Querelle des Femmes."
Many of the works in this vein treat Christine de Pisan as the
"first of our feminists," thus tracing modern feminism all the
way back to the beginning of the fifteenth century.[1]

Recent scholarship, strongly influenced by the feminism
of our own day, perpetuates this way of thinking. In *The Second Sex*, which launched a new wave of feminist speculation
in 1949, Simone de Beauvoir declared that "society has
always been male," that "political power has always been in
the hands of men," and that the "quarrel" between men and
women, accordingly, "will go on as long as men and women
fail to recognize each other as peers." Since "patriarchal society . . . goes back as far as recorded history," as Eva Figes
argued in 1970, it follows that "patriarchal attitudes"—the
belief that women belong in the kitchen, the treatment of
women as instruments of men's pleasure—have a history as
old as history. Strictly speaking, they have no history at all,
since they never change. "In all periods of history," writes
Katharine Rogers in her study of misogyny, "there has been a
dark stream of attacks on women," and the substance of this
indictment, her book leads us to believe, remains unchanged
over the centuries. Joan Kelly's study of the *querelle des
femmes*—the literary controversy about women conducted in
late medieval and early modern Europe—tries to establish a
"400-year-old tradition of women thinking about women and
sexual politics" before the French revolution, in the course of
which "their understanding of misogyny and gender led many
feminists to a universalistic outlook that transcended the
accepted value systems of the time." The early feminists,
beginning with Christine de Pisan, understood that the "sexes
are culturally, and not just biologically, formed," and their
"rewriting of history," according to Kelly, provided an "utterly
feminist . . . critique of culture."[2]

This anachronistic interpretation of an earlier dispute about women, by transforming defenders of women's "honor" into modern feminists, obscures the nature and significance of the *querelle des femmes* and makes it impossible, moreover, to identify what was original and historically unprecedented in feminism itself. Modern feminism, until recently at least, promised not to intensify sexual warfare but to bring about a new era of sexual peace in which men and women could meet each other as equals, not as antagonists. The earlier controversies about women, on the other hand, took sexual antagonism for granted. More precisely, they took for granted the contradiction between love, which rested on sexual equality, and marriage, a hierarchical arrangement in which a wife was expected to submit to her husband's authority. The *querelle des femmes* had its material roots in aristocratic customs governing marriage, which defined marriage as a dynastic institution, not as an expression of sexual attraction. In late medieval and early modern Europe—a society newly conscious of the power of sexual attraction and inclined to surround it, moreover, with an elaborately idealized body of imagery and conventions, to exalt romantic passion as the most intense emotion available to mankind—the contradiction between marriage and passion became almost unbearable. Poetry and satire registered this contradiction and attempted to relieve it with tears and laughter. Until the eighteenth century, however, no one gave much thought to the possibility of overcoming it altogether.

The *querelle des femmes* is usually dated from the second part of the *Roman de la Rose*, written by Jean de Meun between 1275 and 1280. Incongruously grafted onto Guillaume de Lorris's lyrical tribute to courtly love, this celebrated work presented a kind of symposium on love, which juxtaposed various positions and put them in the mouths of stock characters immediately recognizable to a knowledgeable audience. As Pierre Col pointed out in reply to critics of the poem, Jean de Meun spoke through "personnaiges" and "fait chascun personnaige parler selonc qui luy appartient."[3] The highly conventionalized speeches assigned to these characters combined themes drawn from courtly romance with themes drawn from satirical stories of marriage and everyday life (fabliaux) in which young wives and their lovers foil a jealous husband in the attempt to monopolize his wife's affections. The courtly veneration of womanhood had as its obverse a certain uneasiness about female sexuality, which betrayed itself in a deeply rooted conviction of woman's inconstancy. La donna è mobile. Jean de Meun's disputation on love scandalized his audience, in all likelihood, because for the first time it brought courtly lyricism and low comedy together in the same work, thereby hinting at their underlying identity.[4] In deliberately violating the conventional separation of genres, the Roman de la Rose opened the way for the Decameron and the Canterbury Tales. Yet in many ways it looked back to the twelfth century, to the first courtly poets and also to the twelfth-century revival of classical learning— the most important influence on the humanism of Jean de Meun. The courtly lyric itself owed something to classical traditions, the meaning of which, however, medieval authors completely transformed.[5] The recovery of the classics not only revived old arguments, pro and con, about the "art of love" but also encouraged the spirit of disputation in general, exemplified in its most compelling form in Abelard's Sic et Non. The love of contradictions, not the hatred of women, furnished the real inspiration behind the Roman de la Rose. Jean's poem explored the sic et non of love and marriage. Just as Abelard produced arguments on both sides of theological and philosophical questions, Jean de Meun argued both sides of the question of Eros.

Its critics found the poem disrespectful of women, coarse, and obscene. In her *Epistle to the God of Love*, Christine de Pisan demanded that detractors of women be banished from his court. Jean de Montreuil replied with a long defense of the "profound and famous work of Master Jean de Meun." Other worthies entered the fray on both sides. Much of the contention centered on passages—naively assumed by critics and sometimes even by defenders of the poem to represent the opinions of the author himself—that celebrated fecundity and upheld the propagation of the human race as an inescapable obligation enjoined both by nature and by the gods. When Jean's followers claimed that he upheld marriage, condemned adultery, and aimed merely to show young women how to defend themselves against seduction, Christine replied indignantly that his poem addressed itself to those who laid siege to the castle, not to its beleaguered defenders.[6]

The *querelle de la rose* eventually subsided, but the *querelle des femmes* continued for another three centuries. Works like Alain Chartier's *La Belle Dame sans Merci* and the anonymous *Les Quinze Joyes de Mariage*—the latter depicting the misfortunes of a young husband beset with a nagging, extravagant, unfaithful wife—carried the tradition of the *Roman de la Rose* and the *fabliaux* into the fifteenth century. Rabelais's *Gargantua and Pantagruel* is often regarded as having revived it a century later, the discussion of marriage in Book III, according to one author, recalling the "old dispute begun in the *Roman de la Rose*" and at the same time looking ahead to Molière, who allegedly shared with Rabelais the prejudice that a "woman's place is in the home."[7]

Together with works by Boccaccio, Chaucer, and Erasmus, often cited as belonging to the same genre of abusive commentary on women, these stand out as major landmarks in a literary tradition carried on for the most part by minor writers and therefore distinguished by stylized and repetitive arguments on either side. Certain authors seem to have taken part on both sides of the debate—another indication of the stylized, ritualistic quality of the literary abuse and defense of womanhood.[8] In many tracts, as in the *Roman de la Rose* itself—the progenitor of this genre—arguments for and against women appeared side by side. By the end of the sixteenth century, the *querelle des femmes* had degenerated into formulaic diatribes against women, countered by equally conventional and predictable arguments in defense of women. Yet the subjects around which it revolved—jealousy, adultery, and sexual combat—continued to serve as a source of fresh inspiration not only to Molière but also to the Restoration dramatists in England. It was only in the eighteenth century that the old debate about women gave way to a new debate founded on wholly different premises.

Eighteenth-century feminists began to argue for the first time that masculinity and femininity are social conventions alterable by education. Those who took part in the *querelle des femmes* took it for granted, on the other hand, that people grow up into sexual roles. It would never have occurred to them that a woman can be, or ought to be, anything other than what she is—what she is destined to become. They defined virtue as conduct appropriate to one's station, which included social rank and gender. Those who debated the pros and cons of womanhood did not concern themselves with the abstract question of whether nature makes one sex superior to the other. Such a question would have seemed completely meaningless to the medieval and early modern mind.

The issue that presented itself to those times was not whether woman is equal to man in the abstract but rather in what social relationships is she his equal, in what relations his subordinate?

Strictly speaking, the *querelle des femmes* was not a dispute about women at all, but a dispute about marriage. Should a man marry? If he does, does he marry anything but trouble? Do the pleasures of marriage outweigh its innumerable irritations and inconveniences? Do husbands have the right to be jealous of their wives' lovers? Are they justified in accusing the female sex of inconstancy, calculating seductiveness, and insatiable lust? Was it male lust, on the contrary, that lured women into adultery and fornication? Should adultery and fornication be condemned in the first place? Isn't the free union of adulterous lovers morally superior to the forced union of husband and wife? "Antifeminist" invective directed itself not to the abstract question of whether women are naturally submissive, passive, and inferior—issues that figured prominently in later debates about women—but to the concrete miseries and dangers of marriage. Denunciation of women and denunciation of marriage went hand in hand. Satire directed itself not against women as such but against the contrast between their status as lovers and their status as wives.

In marriage, a wife was expected to defer to her husband's judgment and to obey his orders. Marriage meant the end of sexual equality, hence also the end of love. In the words of the arch-"antifeminist" himself, Jean de Meun, "There's no companionship twixt love and siegneury."[9] Heloise advanced the same kind of argument against Abelard's ill-conceived proposal of marriage, "preferring love to wedlock," as she later wrote, "and freedom to chains."[10] The incompatibility of love and marriage was the central premise that underlay both of the literary traditions the juxtaposition of which made up the medieval dialectic of love. Courtly poetry glorified adultery on the grounds that equality, and therefore erotic passion, can have no place in marriage. The stylistic antithesis of courtly romance—the comic satire against marriage exemplified in the *fabliaux* and given lasting expression by Chaucer, Boccaccio, and Rabelais—either deplored or maliciously celebrated the refusal of wives to accept their subordinate status with good grace. Instead of submitting demurely to their fate, wives berate their husbands, dress up in expensive clothes designed to show off their figures, and enjoy love affairs with younger men. The insubordinate wife makes her husband an object of ridicule and crowns her career by crowning him with horns—the climactic indictment of matrimony, to which medieval and early modern satire returned with obsessive interest.

At a time when social ridicule—institutionalized in such popular customs as the *charivari*—served as the most effective sanction with which to enforce everyday morality, the fear of ridicule dominated discussion of marriage. The comic figure of the jealous husband personified this fear. It is he who usually gives voice both to the stock criticism of marriage and to the stock vilification of women; and since he is himself an object of conventional satire, the satire against women also contained a satire against the male in his capacity as householder, husband, and cuckold. Far from giving vent to "antifeminist" prejudices, aristocratic satire rested on criticism of marriage and more specifically of jealousy, rightly believed to dominate relations not founded on the principle of voluntary, reciprocal submission. The courtly lover swears to serve his mistress—a word people of the Middle Ages still used with an awareness of its political overtones—in the same way that a vassal swears homage to his lord. *Frauen-*

dienst becomes the erotic equivalent of feudalism: a bond between the free and equal. The jealous husband, on the other hand, demands from his wife a subordination to which he is legally entitled but which he is powerless to enforce.

One of the most durable among the many misunderstandings surrounding medieval literary traditions is that courtly poetry, in its refined idealization of love, developed in opposition to a "bourgeois" and ecclesiastical literature that made fun of marriage and treated women with contempt. Thus it is said of the Chevalier de la Tour-Landy, one of the fifteenth-century "misogynists" who entered the debate about women, that his attitude was "thoroughly bourgeois as regards the position of women and, no doubt, reflects the viewpoint of a large part of the lesser nobility, which was never closely in touch with the movement of chivalrous gallantry and female supremacy."[11] In his classic study of the *fabliaux*, Joseph Bédier described these ribald narratives as the expression of a "bourgeois Dionysian myth," a bourgeois vision of earthly abundance. According to Bédier, aristocratic exaltation of womanhood gave rise to a contemptuous bourgeois reply, "*préciosité* to *gauloiserie*, the dream to derision, courtesy to villainy, the cult of the lady to . . . bantering scorn and . . . raillery." In their rivalry, each class developed characteristic attitudes about women, formalized in rival genres.[12]

Yet Bédier himself noted that the *fabliaux*, like the courtly lyrics and romances, were composed by wandering scholars, minstrels, and *jongleurs*, not by bourgeois authors, and that they found favor with the same aristocratic audience that delighted in the myth of courtly love. Bédier pointed out that both types of stories, moreover, share important structural features. In both genres, he wrote, the family is "singularly reduced," consisting of the husband, his wife, and her young lover. Nor did it escape his attention that a reader is no more likely to meet a young unmarried girl in the *fabliaux* than in the *chansons d'amour*.[13] Both genres, in other words, deal with illicit love for a lady. If Bédier had allowed himself to speculate about the reasons for this uniformity of content, he would have found it hard to avoid the conclusion that both genres uphold adultery against marriage and that both, indeed, tell the same story. The only difference is that in the comic version, the lovers outwit the stupid, gullible husband, whereas in the courtly version, the forces of social order (marital, ecclesiastical, and dynastic) usually prevail, leaving the lovers to seek union only in death.

It should not surprise us that the aristocratic literature of love, whether comic or courtly, revolved around the triangle composed of the jealous husband, his beautiful young wife, and the wife's lover, often depicted as a kinsman, vassal, or retainer of the husband, as if to highlight the Oedipal rivalries underlying this three-cornered sexual comedy. As long as marital alliances played a central part in the consolidation and transmission of landed property and in the continuity of the aristocratic house or lineage, marriages continued to be arranged without regard to romantic passion or to the wishes of the young. Such conditions naturally discouraged any inclination to identify love with marriage. The aristocratic marriage system, moreover, often paired older husbands with young wives, since men found it hard to marry before coming into an inheritance.[14] Courtly romance and its comic antithesis, the "misogynistic," "antifeminist" satire against marriage, sprang from matrimonial arrangements that required the subordination of wives and children. Literary students of domestic conflict never questioned the necessity of those arrangements, but they insisted that heads of households, especially if they marry high-spirited women much younger than themselves, find it hard to exercise their rightful authority in a just and even-handed way. Instead these men fall prey to jealousy and suspicion. They become either hateful tyrants or figures of fun. If they indulge their wives, they soon regret it. If they beat them, they fare no better in the end. In medieval and early modern satire, physical force merely represents, as usual, the last refuge of failed authority. It gives the jealous husband no comfort. He remains obsessed by the fear—by the certainty—that in spite of his beating and his jealous supervision, his wife will dishonor him. In the end he allows himself to be dominated not by a mistress to whom he has voluntarily sworn submission, not even by an insubordinate, domineering wife, but by his own obsession, which consumes him.

In the hands of a master, the underlying pathos of the jealous patriarch became fully explicit. Thus Shakespeare saw the psychological truth beneath the conventional mockery of marriage and the misogynistic attitudes associated with it: that the misogynist makes himself his own victim. In *Othello*, he raised the jealous husband to the level of a tragic hero. Here and elsewhere, he gave new life to another theme associated with anti-marriage satire, the woman falsely accused. In the satirical tradition, wives do not always outwit their husbands by taking lovers. Sometimes they suffer patiently, like Griselda, under reproaches that have no foundation in fact. Shakespeare endowed Griselda with a tragic dignity in the person of Desdemona or again in Cordelia, another victim of jealous patriarchal authority. A certain spiritual kinship unites these long-suffering wives and daughters and also unites the men who unreasonably accuse them of disloyalty, patriarchs based on the familiar figure of the jealous husband or the more pathetic figure of the father at odds with his favorite daughter. In his eagerness to believe the worst of those who love him, Lear is cousin to Othello.

The *querelle des femmes* unfolded in an age that delighted in dialectics and carried to a high pitch of refinement the art of verbal disputation. Like the tournament—to which it was often compared—stylized disputation sublimated warfare, just as courtly love sublimated lust. On one side, the literary controversy about women owed something to the ritual warfare of the joust: the champions of woman's honor saw themselves as knights riding to her defense against detractors. On the other side, it breathed the air of the schools, where dialecticians sought to overwhelm opponents with dazzling logic and impressive displays of learning. The quarrel about women took the form of a ritual contest in which clearly identifiable disputants take positions inseparable from their social roles. In the *Roman de la Rose*, the most notorious "antifeminist" tirades are delivered not by the author (who never speaks in his own voice) but by the young lover's Friend, by the Jealous Husband, and by another stock figure of medieval satire, the Vieille or Duenna, who teaches young women the ways of the world. The Friend advises the lover, against the precepts of courtly love, to use every artifice in pursuit of his goal and to seize it by force if necessary. The Jealous Husband accuses women of extravagance, vanity, insubordination, and infidelity. He lectures the lover on the dangers of marriage, pointing to the well-documented truth that no woman resists for long (even if she happens to be married to someone else) the siege of a determined lover. He caps the case against marriage by recalling the unhappy history of Heloise and Abelard. Their troubles began when they married, overriding Heloise's better judgment. Abelard's fate—emasculation—awaits every husband: such is the burden of the Jealous Husband's monologue. But that monologue is immediately followed, it should be noted, by a passage in which the Friend draws a different moral, one that contradicts the cynical advice he himself gave earlier. A jealous husband tyrannizes over his wife, the Friend points out, whereas lovers "are emancipated, frank, and free." This explains why love usually dies with marriage: he who once swore himself woman's slave now sets himself up as her lord and master.[15]

The Duenna's coarse, cynical speech, which answers the complaint of the Jealous Husband, consists of advice to young women by a woman of the world. It represents another form of satire on marriage, which takes the wife's side against a husband who tries to monopolize her affections. The Duenna lists all the things a lady has to do in order to find the right kind of lovers. Dress so as to conceal your defects and show off your charms. Wipe your mouth before drinking; don't go to sleep at the table; don't get drunk—for a "drunken woman is without defense." Carry yourself seductively in the street. Avoid poor men and proud men alike. Don't lose yourself in love; calculate. Don't give your heart away, make him pay for it. Don't give it to one man alone: witness the fate of Dido and Medea. All women love the "game" of love and have a right to play it, the Duenna insists; jealous husbands should suffer in silence. "Every female longs for every male, and each gives free consent."[16]

The assertion of woman's sexual freedom and the mockery of marriage, one might suppose, should have commended itself to female readers of the *Roman de la Rose.* It was precisely these passages, however, together with a few others, that provoked the most important criticism of the poem advanced by Christine de Pisan. The entire second half of the *Roman,* she argued—like Ovid's *Art of Love,* on which it was modeled—had no other purpose than to instruct men in the military science of seduction. In Christine's eyes, the poem's libel of womanhood lay in the claim that women not only provoke sexual encounters but seek them so ardently that they can seldom rise to the demands of loyalty or wifely submission. She tried to show that Jean de Meun contradicted himself when he outlined elaborate strategies with which to capture a stronghold allegedly on the verge of surrender. If women are as weak as their detractors claim, why do men devise such complicated schemes to overcome their resistance? In order to enter a captured castle, you don't need to start a war.[17]

Some historians of the *querelle des femmes* claim that the grounds of debate shifted over the centuries. Whereas medieval polemics addressed the question of which sex was superior, seventeenth-century "feminists" advanced the more radical claim that woman is man's equal.[18]

But even the boldest claims advanced in the seventeenth century for the most part still adhered to the old terms of debate. The *querelle des femmes*, refined and elaborated in the writing of the *précieuses*, in the plays of Molière, in Restoration comedy, in the novel of worldliness, and in the heated discussions about women that enlivened the salons of London and Paris, remained a debate about marriage, in which both sides started from the same premise: that marriage is incompatible with sexual equality.[19] This premise could lead to an increasingly cynical defense of adultery or, on the other hand, to a defense of a single life not only for men but for women as well. In the Age of Reason, a number of prominent women joined men in upholding the advantages of independence, and it is the anti-marriage arguments articulated by women that make seventeenth-century "feminism" look modern. The context of those arguments, however, still links them to older traditions.

Consider the claims advanced by the high-minded women who asserted their right to remain single in seventeenth-century England. Most of these women were Catholics or high-church Anglicans unreconciled to the Protestant celebration of married life and resentful of the growing contempt for spinsters. In reply, they sought to restore the moral esteem formerly reserved for virginity. They deplored the dissolution of monasteries in England and sought to provide single women with a substitute for these useful institutions. Mary Ward, a Catholic, established a foundation for single women with the help of Queen Henrietta Maria. She did not deny that "women are to be subjected to their husbands," nor did she question the social conventions according to which "men are head of the church, women are not to administer sacraments, nor preach in public churches." She insisted, however, that women were the intellectual equals of men and that a life devoted to piety and learning had as much value as marriage.[20] "The belief that virginity is the noblest ideal of life did not entirely die with the nunneries," according to one scholar; "in high church circles it survived throughout the 17th century."[21] In the 1630s, two sisters, Anne and Mary Collett, managed to found a kind of Protestant convent at Gedding in Huntingtonshire, in spite of the opposition of their bishop, who advised them to marry in order "that they might not be led into temptation." In a letter written to her uncle in 1631, Anne Collett expressed a strong desire to remain single. "Touching my condition of life, such content do I find, I neither wish nor desire any change in it; but as God may please, with my Parents' leave, to give me grace and strength, that I may spend the remainder of my days without greater encumbrances of this world, which do of necessity accompany a married Estate." In 1641, a Puritan pamphlet demanded a Parliamentary investigation of the "nunnery" established by the Collett sisters.[22]

The most prominent advocate of a Protestant version of monasticism, Mary Astell, noted that "very good Protestants" continued to complain, even at the end of the seventeenth century, that "monasteries were Abolished instead of being Reform'd." She called for the creation of a "monastery or if you will (to avoid giving offence to the scrupulous and injudicious) . . . we will call it a Religious Retirement," designed to provide a "retreat from the World for those who desire that advantage." She ridiculed the widespread fear of "dispeopling the World" and extolled the virtue of a single life.[23] The daughter of a high-church, mercantile family in Newcastle, Astell opposed the admission of occasional conformists to public office, condemned immoral novels and plays, and upheld the divine right of kings. Although she is often mentioned as a precursor of Mary Wollstonecraft, there is no evidence that her writings had any influence on Wollstonecraft; nor is there any reason to endorse the claim that "it was a hundred and fifty years before her vision . . . was fulfilled" by the establishment of the first women's colleges at Oxford and Cambridge.[24] Far from being ahead of her time, she was hopelessly behind it. Her ideas appealed principally to conservatives like John Evelyn, who shared her wish that "at the first Reformation in this Kingdom, some of these demolished Religious Foundations had been spared both for Men and Women; where single persons devoutly inclined might have retired and lived without Reproach, or ensnaring Vows."[25]

It was not only the economic realities underlying matrimonial arrangements that made it difficult for aristocrats and religious conservatives to take a fresh look at marriage and courtship but the persistence of long-established conventions associated with the "art of love" and the verbal battle of the sexes. The courtship ritual of agonistic insult proved so durable and satisfying, as a literary convention, that it must have drawn not only on current experience—which suggested to many observers, in the sixteenth and seventeenth centuries, that match-making had become increasingly cynical and mercenary—but also on ancestral memories of the rivalry underlying all forms of marriage and courtship.[26] In *The Taming of the Shrew*, Shakespeare made the art of sexual insult, elevated to a new level of verbal refinement, bear the whole weight of the dramatic action. Witty exchanges between courting couples figure in many of his other comedies as well. Beaumont and Fletcher used this convention so freely—in *The Woman's Prize, or The Tamer Tame'd* (1611), *The Scornful Lady* (1613), *The Wild Goose Chase* (1621), and *Rule a Wife and Have a Wife* (1624)—that their comedies created a whole vogue of plays built on the "combat between the sexes," as one critic describes it, having as central characters the "wild gallant and his witty mistress" and taking a "cynical attitude toward marriage and sex."[27] In Restoration comedy, the ritual antagonism of the sexes becomes a matter of obsessive fascination. In Congreve's *Love for Love*, Angelica replies to those who abuse women with the familiar argument that men, not women, initiate sexual hostilities by professing a devotion they do not feel. " 'Tis an unreasonable accusation, that you lay upon our sex: you tax us with injustice, only to cover up your own want of merit. . . . Men are generally hypocrites and infidels, they pretend to worship, but have neither zeal nor faith." A favorite plot, used by one Restoration playwright after another, depicts a woman-hater and shrew-tamer himself tamed by a witty woman, in the course of verbal duels that rehearse the conventional themes of sexual antagonism and misogyny. In Cavendish's *Humorous Lovers* (1677), Boldman, a self-professed "despiser of Love," advises a friend to avoid that "sickly, whining, and unmanly humour; a Man is good for nothing while he has the fit upon him." "I fear the wed-lock Ring," he goes on, "more than the Bear do's the Ring in his Nose. Oh! the torment to be tied to the stake of Matrimony, and to be baited all the dayes of a Man's life by a Wife." Here, as in Dryden's *Secret Love*, the misogynist eventually falls in love with a witty heroine, "so horribly much," in the words of Dryden's Celadon, "that contrary to my own Maxims, I think in my conscience I could marry you." Heartfree, the protagonist of John Vanbrugh's *Provok'd Wife* (1697), delivers himself of a tirade against marriage, with the usual references to Eve, to women's "tricks," and to their pride, vanity, covetousness, indiscretion, and malice. When he fails to make a misogynist of his friend Constant, Heartfree resolves to provide him with the skills with which to bring his mistress to bed. "Since I can't bring you quite off of her, I'll endeavor to bring you quite on, for a whining lover is the damnedest companion upon earth." In the end, Heartfree himself succumbs to Bellinda, not without reminding himself that marriage is a lottery, a "great leap in the dark."[28]

Colley Cibber's *Careless Husband* (1704), a comedy built entirely around the erotic battle of wits, shows how little the terms of debate had altered over the centuries. Lady Easy, unhappily married to a womanizer, makes speeches that combine criticism of current marital fashions with the age-old accusation that men have reduced the art of love to a technique of sexual conquest. "Nowadays one hardly ever hears of such a thing as a man of quality in love with the woman he would marry. To be in love now is only having a design upon a woman, a modish way of declaring war against her virtue." The advice given to a naive young lover by her husband and his fellow-tutor, Lord Foppington, shows the justice of this complaint. "Courage is the whole mystery of love," according to Lord Foppington, "and more use than conduct is in war." Sir Charles Easy believes that "women are only cold . . . from the modesty or fear of those that attack 'em." The courtship of Lady Betty Modish by their "pupil," Lord Morelove, consists of verbal fencing. Morelove learns to play the part of a misogynist, not very eloquently imitating his masters in vituperation: "The mischiefs skulking behind a beauteous form give no warning." Lady Betty, a coquette who believes (or professes to believe) that "sincerity in love is as much out of fashion as sweet snuff," sees through Morelove's disguise without difficulty. Her verbal triumphs elicit Lord Foppington's admiration. "Your ladyship pushed like a fencing master; that last thrust was a *coup de grâce*, I believe." Only when Sir Charles convinces her that Morelove is determined to have nothing further to do with her does Lady Betty, regretting her "giddy woman's slights," renounce "gallantry" and apologize to her long-suffering lover. Meanwhile Sir Charles has undergone a similar change of heart. Finding that his wife has suffered his own infidelities with the patience of a Griselda—infidelities he had imagined undiscovered—he promises constancy henceforth.

> In all my past experience of the sex I found even among the better sort so much of folly, pride, malice, passion, and irresolute desire, that I concluded thee but of the foremost rank, and therefore scarce worthy my concern. But thou has stirred me with so severe a proof of thy exalted virtue, it gives me wonder equal to my love.[29]

As always, the example of a virtuous wife counters the record of woman's wiles, shames men who abuse women, and brings the *querelle des femmes* to a provisional but satisfyingly symmetrical resolution, in which both sexes admit their faults and vow to mend their ways.

In emphasizing the persistence of certain themes and conventions associated with the ritual battle of the sexes, I do not mean to deny that every age adapts old conventions to its own purposes. Thus in seventeenth-century England, many playwrights revived conventional satire against courtly love in order to ridicule the vogue of platonic love, itself a revival of courtly traditions, introduced by Henrietta Maria in the 1630s.[30] In France, the countercourtly tradition served to enliven ridicule of the *précieuses*, many of whom celebrated platonic attachments. But the comic playwrights and novelists of the seventeenth century, French and English alike, directed most of their criticism, as did the *précieuses* themselves, against a more important and in the long run more threatening object than platonic love: the competing sexual morality that was beginning to emerge among the middle classes. As merchants and professional men grew more wealthy and self-assertive, more insistent than before on the need for strict standards of sexual propriety in marriage, and more emphatic in their attacks on fashionable license, aristocratic satirists launched a counterattack on middle-class marriage. The critique of sexual jealousy and jealous husbands, always an important ingredient both in the courtly tradition and in the satire it called forth in rebuttal, now took on broader implications as part of a new ethic of worldly civility, advanced in opposition to the sexual enslavement of women allegedly practiced in bourgeois circles and to the unenlightened sexual attitudes among the more rustic members of the nobility. Aristocrats in the age of Louis XIV regarded a rational code of sexual morality as one of their principal achievements. But in their eagerness to distinguish themselves not only from their social inferiors but also from the "barbarous" past, they minimized their indebtedness to earlier traditions. The concept of honor, always central to an aristocratic code of conduct, continued to dominate speculation about love and marriage in the seventeenth and eighteenth centuries. A revised ideal of honor—not, as some interpreters have argued, a shift from an external system of emotional regulation to an internal one—informed the new code of "civility" and the aristocratic feminism so often associated with it.[31] Thus the "terrible indictment of marriage" drawn up by the "feminist logicians" of the salons, as one historian refers to it, carried one step further the traditional mockery of jealous husbands.[32] A wife's infidelity should no longer be considered a disgrace to her husband, according to the *précieuses*. Jealousy itself was the disgrace; and even if a husband found himself faced with a rival, his honor lay in avoiding any public display of emotion. The conventions now widely accepted in polite society accounted a husband "wiser when he knows how to suffer than when he has found the means of avenging himself" on an unfaithful wife and her lover.

> It is the first lesson one gives to those who marry, to defend themselves against suspicion and jealousy. . . . We live without constraint, even before our husbands, and . . . they do not dare to exclude or rebuke us. A husband has to put up with the most hateful countenances, approve the desires and designs of his wife, and know how to bend to debauches and diversions, and discommode himself or interrupt his own affairs sooner than obstructing his wife's parties or interfering with her walks or conversations.[33]

The *précieuses* not only denounced jealousy in husbands but insisted that a woman should not be expected to submit to the advances of a man who disgusted her. They condemned men who kept their wives pregnant all the time and defended women's right to remain single, on the grounds that love seldom survives the "long enslavement" of marriage. Sappho, the heroine of Madeleine de Scudéry's novel *Le Grand Cyrus*, knows men, she says, "who deserve my esteem and could even win a part of my friendship," but as soon as she thinks of them as husbands, she finds that she "regards them as masters so near to becoming tyrants that it is impossible for me not to hate them from that instant."[34] In another novel based on the ideas of the *précieuses*, one of the characters finds it impossible to conceive of a "tyranny in the world more cruel, more severe, more unbearable than that of these shackles lasting right up to the tomb." A wife, she declares,

> has to support an insupportable thing; and—what, to my mind, is the epitome of the tyranny of marriage—she is obliged, I say, to take to her frozen breast the ardors of her husband, to endure the caresses of a man who displeases her, who is horrible to her mind and heart. She finds herself in his arms, she receives his kisses, and no matter what obstacle her aversion and pain can discover, she is constrained to submit and to receive the law of the conqueror.[35]

The *précieuses* attacked the double standard of sexual morality by demanding the same privileges for women that men wished to monopolize. Bourgeois morality, on the other hand—however imperfectly realized in practice—implied a very different kind of attack on the double standard: monogamy for men and women alike. Modern feminism, already implicit in the new conception of domestic life that was beginning to emerge in the seventeenth and eighteenth centuries, attempted to reconcile marriage with sexual equality. From a worldly point of view, this was a utopian undertaking. Criticism of marriage resembled Catholic criticism of monasticism. It assumed the immutability of the institution under attack. Just as writers like Erasmus and Rabelais had denounced corrupt and lascivious monks as bitterly as any Protestant, but without calling into question the institution of monasticism itself, critics of marriage—often the very same writers—took it for granted that marriage would always represent a union of fortunes and lineages, not the union of lovers, and that it would therefore lead, in the normal course of things, to emotional suffering on both sides, to adultery and sexual intrigue, to jealousy and suspicion, and to the contest for sexual supremacy, in short, the nuances of which these writers described, at their best, with such an abundance of carefully observed psychological details.

Feminism, beginning with Poullain de la Barre and Mary Wollstonecraft, rested on the belief that social institutions can be redesigned according to principles accessible to human reason. Just as science promised control over nature, economics and a new understanding of history promised control over social relations, hitherto shaped by accident and historical drift. Even the relations between men and women, seemingly ordained by biology, could be reordered once they were perceived as the product of custom, "prejudice," law, and education. Such was the hope that gave birth to modern feminism: a new sexual dispensation based on human intelligence and rational design, not on the irrational irrelevance of gender.

More specifically, the climate of opinion in which feminist ideas took root was shaped by the Cartesian revolution in philosophy, quite directly in the case of Poullain de la Barre. The Cartesian proclamation of the mind's independence of the body made it possible to argue that mind has no sex, as feminists used to say. According to one account of the unceasing, unchanging controversy between men and women, as it mistakenly appears to so many modern historians, this was one of "two directly opposite lines of thought" that had persisted "throughout the centuries," the other being the dogma that "woman's special province is the home."[36] In fact, however, the disembodied character of mind is a distinctively modern idea, as is the disembodied, presocial conception of selfhood according to which individuals owe nothing to society, flourish fully formed in a state of nature, and enter into the social contract only to secure the inalienable rights they already enjoy. Only when men and women began to abstract mind from body and the self from its social roles was it possible to envision a fundamental modification of the conventions hitherto governing courtship, marriage, and the position of women in society.

One other influence on feminism might be mentioned: the waning of the play-element in the battle of the sexes. It is the highly stylized character of this competition, more than anything else, that distinguishes modern sexual polemics from the "age-old game of attraction and repulsion played by young men and girls," celebrated both in the courtly tradition and, more robustly, in the aristocratic tradition of erotic comedy that found expression in the *fabliaux*, on the Restoration stage, and in the works of Rabelais and Molière. Only when "civilization as a whole becomes more serious," in Huizinga's words—when not only "law and war, commerce, technics and science" but love itself "lose touch with play; and even ritual . . . seems to share the process of dissociation"—does the old game of love begin to look deadly serious.[37] At that point, it becomes difficult to remember that it was ever anything else.

NOTES

1. Francis Baumal, *Le féminisme au temps de Molière* (Paris, n.d. [ca. 1923]), 8–10; Blanche Hinman Dow, *The Varying Attitude toward Women in French Literature of the Fifteenth Century* (New York, 1936), 48; Gustave Reynier, *La femme au XVIIe siècle* (Paris, 1929), 2–3. See also Theodore Joran, *Les féministes avant le féminisme* (Paris, 1910).

2. Simone de Beauvoir, *The Second Sex*, H. M. Parshley, trans. (New York, 1961), 65, 676; Eva Figes, *Patriarchal Attitudes* (New York, 1970), 25; Katharine M. Rogers, *The Troublesome Helpmate: A History of Misogyny in Literature* (Seattle, 1966), ix; Joan Kelly, "Early Feminist Theory and the *Querelle des Femmes*, 1400–1789," *Signs* 8 (1982), 5, 7, 18, 20.

3. Francis Lee Utley, *The Crooked Rib: An Analytical Index to the Argument about Women in English and Scots Literature to the End of the Year 1568* (Columbus, Ohio, 1944), 20. On the *Roman de la Rose* and the controversy it set off, see Alan M. F. Gunn, *The Mirror of Love* (Lubbock, Tex., 1952); Lionel J. Friedman, " 'Jean de Meung,' Antifeminism, and 'Bourgeois Realism,' " *Modern Philology* 57 (1959), 13–23; Lula McDowell Richardson, *The Forerunners of Feminism in French Literature of the Renaissance from Christine de Pisan to Marie de Gournay* (Baltimore, 1929); Dow, *Women in French Literature;* Marguerite Favier, *Christine de Pisan: Muse des cours souveraines* (Lausanne, 1967); and Charles Frederick Ward, "The Epistles on the *Romance of the Rose* and Other Documents in the Debate" (Ph.D. diss., University of Chicago, 1911). I am indebted to Vivian Folkenflik for help in translating key documents in the Ward collection from the Old French.

4. On the separation of styles, see Erich Auerbach, *Mimesis: The Representation of Reality in Western Literature*, Willard Trask, trans. (Princeton, N.J., 1953), especially ch. 9.

5. C. S. Lewis, *The Allegory of Love* (Oxford, 1936). For a sampling of the vast body of scholarship on courtly love, see Moshe Lazar, *Amour courtois et fin' amors dans la littérature du XIIe siècle* (Paris, 1964); John C. Moore, *Love in Twelfth-Century France* (Philadelphia, 1972); A. J. Denomy, *The Heresy of Courtly Love* (New York, 1947); F. X. Newman, ed., *The Meaning of Courtly Love* (Binghamton, N.Y., 1967); Aldo D. Scaglione, *Nature and Love in the Late Middle Ages* (Berkeley, Calif., 1963); and Denis de Rougemont, *Love in the Western World*, Montgomery Belgion, trans. (New York, 1956).

6. "Christine's Reply to Pierre Col" (in Ward, "Epistles on the *Romance of the Rose*"), lines 676–747.

7. For a useful corrective to this view of Rabelais, see M. A. Screech, *The Rabelaisian Marriage* (London, 1958), who shows that the *Tiers Livre* cannot be reduced "to the trivial status of an admittedly learned intervention into the *Querelle des Femmes* on the side of extreme antifeminism" (p. 2).

8. Thus Edward Gosynhill, to whom is usually attributed the scurrilous diatribe against women *The School House of Women* (1541), replied to *The School House* a few years later in *The Praise of All Women*. In some works—for instance, in C. Pyrre's *Praise and Dispraise of Women, Very Fruitful to the Well Disposed Mind, and Delectable to the Readers Thereof* (ca. 1563)—arguments for and against women appeared side by side.

9. *The Romance of the Rose*, Harry W. Robbins, trans. (New York, 1962), lines 8452–53.

10. *The Letters of Abelard and Héloise*. Betty Radice, trans. (Harmondsworth, 1974), 114.

11. Raymond Lincoln Kilgour, *The Decline of Chivalry* (Cambridge, Mass., 1937), 116. "The bourgeois temperament," according to Kilgour (p. 358), "is at odds with the refinements of courtly love." See also Helen Waddell, *The Wandering Scholars* (London, 1927), 198, 210, in which Jean de Meun is described as "the *vrai bourgeois.*"

12. Joseph Bédier, *Les fabliaux: Etudes de littérature populaire et d'histoire littéraire du moyen âge* (Paris, 1925), 363–65.

13. Ibid., 322, 370, 378, 382, 385, 392.

14. Georges Duby, *Medieval Marriage*, Elborg Forster, trans. (Baltimore, 1978), 3–15, and "The 'Youth' in 12th-Century Aristocratic Society," in Fredric L. Cheyette, ed., *Lordship and Community in Medieval Europe* (New York, 1968), 198–209; J. Hajnal, "European Marriage Patterns in Perspective," in D. V. Glass and D. E. C. Eversley, eds., *Population in History* (London, 1965), 101–43.

15. *Romance of the Rose*, lines 9413–23; for the speeches in question, see lines 7231–10,005 (the Friend); lines 8464–9360 (the Jealous Husband); and lines 12,541–14,546 (the Duenna).

16. Ibid., lines 14,029–30.

17. "Epistle of the God of Love" (in Ward, "Epistles on the *Romance of the Rose*"), lines 348–406.

18. Richardson, *Forerunners of Feminism*, 155; Emile Telle, *L'Oeuvre de Marguerite d'Angoulême, Reine de Navarre, et la querelle des femmes* (Geneva, 1969), 379–80; Marjorie Henry Ilsley, *A Daughter of the*

Renaissance: Marie le Jars de Gournay, Her Life and Works (The Hague, 1963), 201 and passim; Jacob Bouten, *Mary Wollstonecraft and the Beginnings of Female Emancipation in France and England* (Amsterdam, [1923]), 22–23.

19. On the seventeenth-century controversy about women and marriage— the writings of the *précieuses* in particular—see Baumal, *Le féminisme au temps de Molière;* Reynier, *La Femme au XVIIe siècle;* S. A. Richards, *Feminist Writers of the Seventeenth Century* (London, 1914); Carolyn C. Lougee, *Le Paradis des Femmes: Women, Salons, and Social Stratification in Seventeenth-Century France* (Princeton, N.J., 1976); Jean-Michel Pelous, *Amour précieux, amour galant, 1654–1675: Essai sur la répresentation de l'amour dans la littérature et la société mondaine* (Paris, 1980); Hilda L. Smith, *Reason's Disciples: Seventeenth-Century English Feminists* (Urbana, Ill., 1982); Peter Brooks, *The Novel of Worldliness* (Princeton, N.J., 1969).

20. Florence M. Smith, *Mary Astell* (New York, 1916), 62–63, note 37.

21. Ibid., 63.

22. Ibid., 64–66.

23. Ibid., 23, 52.

24. Ibid., 76. Smith herself admits that "there seems no proof that Mary Astell's writings had any direct influence on Mary Wollstonecraft" (p. 165). Cf. Hilda Smith, *Reason's Disciples,* 207: "Astell's writings . . . apparently had no direct influence on later feminist thinkers." One reason for this, surely—although Astell's admirers ignore it, and indeed persistently try to link her ideas to a later feminist tradition in spite of their own evidence—is that her monastic ideal of education was of little use in the world of the eighteenth and nineteenth centuries, in which education commended itself as preventive exposure to the world, not as a refuge from it.

25. Smith, *Mary Astell,* 74.

26. All over the world, peasant cultures have observed the changing seasons with games and festivals in which groups of young men and women exchange playful insults. In ancient China, these "courteous rivalries" celebrated the "imperious law of union to which [the sexes] were subject," according to Marcel Granet. "But, as representatives of their sex and their clan, weighted with the spirit of the soil, full of domestic pride and sexual egoism, [men and women] felt themselves at first to be rivals. The courteous struggle which was to bring them together opened with a tone of bravado and mistrust." Rhymed cou-

plets, "invented to suit the rhythm of the dance" and flung back and forth "according to the rules of traditional improvisation," elaborated a "whole cycle of venerable analogies." At the feasts of Demeter and Apollo in ancient Greece, "men and women chanted songs of mutual derision"; and this ritual, in the opinion of Johan Huizinga, "may have given rise to the literary theme of the diatribe against womankind." Even in western Europe, the ceremonial rivalry of the sexes, conducted by organized groups of young men and women, continued well into the nineteenth century to play a large part in peasant courtship, itself still linked to seasonal festivities organized in large part by sexually segregated peer groups. Festivals celebrated sexual fecundity in the context of seasonal change—the reawakening of the land in the spring, the fall harvest—but surrounded the union of the sexes with reminders of their opposition: verbal insults, games pitting men against women, and masquerades in which men and women exchanged roles for the purpose of satire and ridicule.

This ritual antagonism of the sexes, which seems to be a universal feature of the neolithic village culture that persists in some peasant societies right down to our own day, reveals a sense of life as the conflict of opposites. A search for the foundations of this antagonism would take us back to the dawn of culture itself. See Marcel Granet, *Chinese Civilization*, Kathleen E. Innes and Mabel R. Brailsford, trans. (New York, 1930), 159–64; Johan Huizinga, *Homo Ludens* (Boston, 1955), 68, 122; Edward Shorter, *The Making of the Modern Family* (New York, 1975), 121–46; Frank J. Warnke, *Versions of Baroque: European Literature in the 17th Century* (New Haven, Conn., 1972), 92–93.

27. John H. Wilson, *The Influence of Beaumont and Fletcher on Restoration Drama* (Columbus, Ohio, 1928), 116–17. See also John Wilcox, *The Relation of Molière to Restoration Comedy* (New York, 1938), 200–201, and John Harrington Smith, *The Gay Couple in Restoration Comedy* (Cambridge, Mass., 1948), 9–13. The following three examples come from Smith's engaging analysis of this theme: Congreve (p. 157), Cavendish (pp. 53–54), and Dryden (p. 56).

28. John Vanbrugh, *The Provoked Wife*, Curt A. Zimansky, ed. (Lincoln, Neb., 1969), 27–28 (act II, scene 1, lines 155–82), 32 (act II, scene 1, lines 304–07, 107 (act V, scene 5, line 67).

29. Colley Cibber, *The Careless Husband*, William W. Appleton, ed. (Lincoln, Neb., 1966), 31 (act II, scene 1, lines 91–95), 43 (act II, scene 2, lines 218–20), 45 (act II, scene 2, lines 285–86), 60 (act III, lines 345–46), 65 (act III, lines 476–77), 66 (act III, lines 497–98), 113 (act V, scene 7, lines 184–89), 118 (act V, scene 7, lines 317–26).

30. Smith, *The Gay Couple*, ch. 2; see also Kathleen M. Lynch, *'The Social Mode of Restoration Comedy* (New York, 1926), ch. 5; Jefferson Butler Fletcher, *"Précieuses* at the Court of Charles I," *Journal of Comparative Literature* 1 (1903), 120–53; and Fletcher, *The Religion of Beauty in Women* (New York, 1911).

31. Norbert Elias, *The Civilizing Process: The History of Manners*, Edmund Jephcott, trans. (New York, 1978) argues that the new "civility" reflected the internalization of social constraints and, more generally, a "renunciation of instinctual gratification" (p. 134).

32. Baumal, *Le féminisme au temps de Molière*, 37, 92. In Baumal's view, no "modern George Sand" stated the case against marriage "with more vigor or apparent logic." *Préciosité* had become *"un veritable foyer de révendications féministes"* (p. 49). Madeleine de Scudéry in particular, with her "spirit of independence" and her "strong taste for liberty"— whose "disdain for marriage" rested on "an extreme concern for personal liberty"—"appears to deserve the name of feminist in the modern sense of the word" (pp. 77–80).

33. Baumal (ibid., 27–29), quoting from the seventeenth-century novel by the Abbé de Pure, *La prétieuse, ou les mystères des ruelles*—a satire of preciosity that nevertheless gave an accurate account, according to Baumal, of what emancipated women were talking about at the time.

34. Quoted in Baumal, *Le féminisme au temps de Molière*, 77–80.

35. Bouten, *Mary Wollstonecraft*, 4–7.

36. Ibid.

37. Huizinga, *Homo Ludens*, 122, 134.

2

The Mysteries of Attraction

The author of a number of admirable books, not a few of which deal with the emerging ideal of romantic love in early modern art and literature, Jean H. Hagstrum has surpassed himself in *Esteem Enlivened by Desire: The Couple from Homer to Shakespeare* (1992), which ranges over more than ten centuries (amply fulfilling the promise of its subtitle) in search of a usable past—an "available heritage concerning the loving couple." To some extent he has also reversed himself, since he now seeks to correct the impression left by his earlier studies, that romantic love came to be associated with marriage only in the modern world. His new book contests this widely accepted interpretation, which Hagstrum attributes to the belated discovery that "love and marriage do not always go together like a horse and carriage." Ever since this disconcerting fact "dawned on us disillusioned moderns . . . it has been a continuing scholarly preoccupation to discover just when romantic love came into Western culture." The prevailing consensus—that it came relatively late (in the cruder version of this thesis, only with the "rise of the middle class")—issues decidedly bedraggled, if not altogether demolished, from this determined assault.

Hagstrum does not deny that many authors, both classical and Christian, took a disparaging view of marriage, emphasizing the wife's subordination, the dangerous power of female sexuality, and the incompatibility of sexual passion with the mundane ends marriage was meant to serve. Xenophon spoke for a longstanding tradition in the ancient world when he defined the purpose of marriage as legitimate offspring and the maintenance of the household economy. In the Christian world, an equally strong tradition viewed marriage as an acceptable but hardly exalted alternative to sexual promiscuity, morally much inferior to virginity. Sexual passion had its champions, of course, but it was thought unsuitable for man and wife. In ancient Greece, it was associated with love between men and boys; in the Middle Ages, with adulterous love between men and women. Hagstrum's thesis is not impaired by the recognition that married love had very little place in the dominant tradition of Western patriarchy.

His claim, though it is supported by an imposing structure of erudition, is more modest: that a countertradition, already present in Homer's account of the homecoming that concludes the *Odyssey*, encouraged a "softening of male power in patriarchy," hedged in that power with "civilizing limitations," idealized marriage as the union of desire and esteem, and held up sexual equality as the precondition of erotic friendship. Hagstrum thinks this "vision of marital love," in a culture that has long been supposed to be without it, owed a good deal to the influence of women, which made itself felt, even in works written by men, in the insight that Eros could be a "force for civility" as well as disruption. From the beginning, it would seem, the West was able to imagine that marriage might rest on sexual attraction and mutual respect, instead of on the sexual subordination that was taken as the norm elsewhere in the world.

Imagination was often at odds with practice, to be sure, but we should not therefore conclude that married love was to be found only in works of art. A play like Aristophanes' *Lysistrata*, Hagstrum argues, would have meant nothing to its audience "had not the *oikos* [the Greek household] been a place much desired by both men and women." That wives could resort to a sexual strike as a form of political protest implied, in the words Hagstrum borrows from Sir Kenneth Dover, that "the marital relationship was much more important in people's actual lives than we would have inferred simply from our knowledge of the law."

The "erotic ideal"—the union of esteem and sexual desire—deserves to be considered "one of the great achievements of Western culture," according to Hagstrum. "But that union did not come easily," he adds. "Esteem had to be divorced from an all-male contest, and sexuality from the stigma of sin or excess." The first of these developments could have occurred only in a culture willing to countenance the possibility that women (and more particularly wives) were good for something besides reproduction and household labor. As for the second, it received support from the tradition of Christian naturalism, as Hagstrum calls it—the refusal to condemn matter as evil or to equate salvation with a dis-embodied spirituality—which tempered the fear of sexuality that was also present (even dominant) in Christianity. The central importance of the Incarnation, in Christian doctrine, always stood in the way of Platonizing and gnosticizing influences that might otherwise have aligned Christianity with those religions that aspire to Nirvana, the extinction of desire. In Christianity as well as Judaism, the love of God was often evoked with an abundance of sexual imagery, the effect of which was not only to displace or sublimate sexual desire but also to give it a certain legitimacy.

Hagstrum's open and unapologetic admiration for West-ern achievements, it hardly needs to be said, goes against the current grain. A man of irenic temper, Hagstrum prefers to emphasize his obligations to other scholars rather than his objections to their work; so it is left mostly to a reviewer to point out that his own work takes issue not merely with prevailing interpretations of the history of love but, at a deeper level, with the whole trend of recent scholarship in the humanities. Although he is clearly sympathetic to femi-nism, he does not subscribe to the kind of feminism that sees nothing in history except the eternal oppression of women and swallows up all distinctions, all cultural variations, in the one all-encompassing, undifferentiated, monolithic category of "patriarchy." Hagstrum's work likewise stands firmly opposed to the cynicism (which runs through so much of the revisionist scholarship on the Renaissance, for example) that seeks to reduce every expression of idealism to the self-inter-ested pursuit of power. Far more worldly than those who aspire to cosmopolitan status by importing their ideas from Paris, he is undismayed by the gap between ideals and reality, often taken to signify the irrelevance of ideals, because he recognizes their power to criticize and even alter reality. His book deals with "our literary and artistic heritage," not with "historical reality as such," but he does not make the current assumption that art has no connection with reality at all or, alternately, that reality represents nothing more than the "social construction" of artists and critics. He rejects the notion that literary works never refer to anything beyond themselves and that it is pointless, therefore, to expect moral instruction from a work of art.

When he refers to art and literature as our "heritage," Hagstrum reduces to a single word everything that distinguishes him from current fashion. He sees the past as a source of moral wisdom, not just as a record of follies presumably outgrown in our more enlightened (if disillusioned) age. He believes in the "ethical imagination," the exercise of which demands that "we respond correctly and historically when we weigh alternatives, suspend easy belief, and project the dynamics of a work of art into a future that reaches out to our own situation." This procedure carries the danger of reading the past too much in the light of present concerns, and Hagstrum does not always avoid it. There are times when his view of history takes on a Whiggish tinge, as when he congratulates Boccaccio for writing stories that are "modern in feeling," deplores the way in which medieval conventions continued, during the Renaissance, to act as a "dragging, traditional chain on . . . progress," or complains that *The Tempest* (almost alone among Shakespeare's plays in upholding a very orthodox, unimaginative view of marriage) "does not put Shakespeare on the frontier of the emergent." An insistently moralizing criticism, as is well known, can interfere with our willingness to take imaginative works on their own terms. Thus Hagstrum misses the satiric intent behind Boccaccio's depiction of the conventional marriage between ill-assorted couples and makes him out to be a reformer instead, the author of an "attack" on the institution of arranged marriage. Admirers of Boccaccio's artistry are likely to be put off by Hagstrum's observation that the *Decameron*, notwithstanding its "modern" feeling, "falls short of [upholding] a satisfying ethical norm." Yet this ethical interrogation of a text, even if the norm in question is too much defined by the "emergent," is vastly preferable to a style of criticism that reflects ethical judgment as completely beside the point.

Hagstrum's literary history of romantic love, because it seeks ethical guidance from the past and not just a better understanding of our ancestors' foibles, amounts also to a defense of romantic love, written with a heartbreaking awareness that lifelong marriage no longer serves as the standard to which erotic practice ought to aspire. Not only marriage but romantic love itself has fallen out of favor. Love at first sight, we are told again and again, provides a shaky basis for marriage. Shared hobbies and tastes, a mutual commitment to compromise, and a willingness to admit that things never stay the same are more likely to endure when passion cools. Lovers should not demand too much of each other. They must allow for the possibility that one of them will probably outgrow the other. To expect fidelity, permanence, undying attachment is to court disappointment. Friendship, homosexual or heterosexual, seems more reliable to us than love, just because it is less demanding and intense. Friendship easily coexists with sex (these days, at least with safe sex) but not with Eros, the "decoration of sexual impulse by art and thought." We like our sexual impulse unadorned, put securely in its place among the "facts of life."

Sex with us is a science, while art and thought have turned to other themes, including the inevitable misunderstandings between men and women, their essential incompatibility, the instability of all attachments, and the unreliability of everything in the world except sharp, small, immediate, and more or less interchangeable pleasures.

Even the "joy of sex" is now shadowed by AIDS. The sense of sexuality as a dangerous, dark, and unpredictable presence in human life—all the more so in its "decorated" forms—has returned to us in full force. The idea that anything so disruptive could lead to lasting relationships—that Eros could be a stabilizing, let alone a civilizing influence—strikes us as a consummate piece of mystification. One hears talk, more wistful than ironic, about the wisdom of arranged marriages—all in all, it is said, a better solution than romance to the intractable problem of male-female union.

To explain the twentieth-century revulsion against romantic love lies beyond the scope of Hagstrum's enterprise, already ambitious enough without this added burden. The hint of an explanation, however, lies in his very formulation of the romantic ideal. The elaboration of the sexual impulse in works of art, he observes, makes us "understand that the passion aroused early and mysteriously carries over into a calm and fruitful married life." Elsewhere he speaks of the "notion that suddenly and mysteriously induced erotic love . . . brings long satisfactions to the couple and also to most of those who witness its formation and wish it well." It is precisely the belief that a "sudden, overwhelming attraction" establishes "unshakable bonds" that the modern mind (or is it the postmodern mind?) finds so shocking. The assertion that this process operates "mysteriously," far from reassuring us, seems to clinch the case against romantic love. We dislike a mystery. We crave what we can control—even if the price we pay for control is drastic shrinkage of our imaginative and emotional horizon.

3

The Suppression of Clandestine Marriage in England: The Marriage Act of 1753

"We deprive ourselves in order to maintain our integrity, we economize in our health, our capacity for enjoyment, our emotions; we save ourselves for something, not knowing for what. And this constant suppression of natural instincts gives us the quality of refinement. . . . Why don't we get drunk? . . . Why don't we fall in love with a different person every month? . . . Thus we strive more toward avoiding pain than seeking pleasure. And the extreme case are people like ourselves who chain themselves together for life and death, who deprive themselves and pine for years so as to remain faithful, and who probably wouldn't survive a catastrophe that robbed them of their beloved."

SIGMUND FREUD TO MARTHA BERNAYS, 1883[1]

According to the canon law of the Middle Ages, engagements to marry, especially if they were followed by sexual intercourse, were as binding as marriage itself. Ecclesiastical courts repeatedly ruled that "precontracts," if witnessed by two observers, might invalidate a later marriage, even a marriage of many years' standing. This judgment may seem arbitrary and irrational by modern standards, but it was completely consistent with the view that an exchange of binding promises and physical union were the essential elements of marriage, not the publication of banns, parental consent, clerical intervention, or even, indeed, the presence of witnesses. Because it upheld marriage as an antidote to lust, the Catholic church made it easy to marry and almost impossible to obtain a divorce.[2]

In the sixteenth century the canon law of marriage came under increasingly vigorous criticism from intellectuals, moralists, reformers, and public officials. Both Catholic and Protestant critics proposed, in effect, a whole new conception of marriage, one that stressed companionship rather than carnal union—the relief of man's loneliness rather than the relief of concupiscence. Catholic critics of the canonical doctrines did not go so far as to maintain, with Luther and Calvin, that marriage was ordained in Paradise (rather than after and because of the Fall), but they were as vehement as Protestant writers in preferring marriage to monasticism, in praising the spiritual dignity of marriage, and in condemning ecclesiastical interference with it—that "tyrannical presumption," as Rabelais put it, which led priests and monks, unmarried themselves, to "meddle with, obtrude upon, and thrust their sickles into, harvests of secular business."[3] Sharing a common aversion to asceticism, Catholic humanists and Protestant reformers came to similar conclusions about marriage—that it was better to struggle actively with the world and its temptations than to retreat into the artificial peace of the cloister; that it was good for the industrious citizen to work at his calling, to set aside goods, reputation, and the well-being of his children against his old age; and that marriage, accordingly, should be revered as the very basis of the social order and at the same time its model—a miniature commonwealth, as preachers and pamphleteers never tired of repeating.

Because they stressed the importance of compatibility between husband and wife, these upholders of marriage condemned both "enforced marriage"—marriages arranged by parents against their children's wishes—and at the other extreme, marriages contracted without parental consent. The latter, they believed, too often rested on passion rather than reason, impulse rather than foresight.[4] Since they insisted on the importance of parental consent, the humanist-Protestant writers on marriage found themselves at odds with the canon law doctrine of precontracts, according to which the consent of parents was incidental to the formation of a valid union. In their propaganda against the canon law they broadened the definition of "clandestine marriage" to include not only marriages to which witnesses were lacking but marriages without parental consent; all such unions they condemned on principle.

In one of his colloquies Erasmus, appealing as he so often does to the memory of an earlier and uncorrupted Christianity, complains that although "it was the Custom in old Times to have the consent of Parents," monks and priests now "undertake to justify a Marriage between a Boy and a Girl, though without the Privity, and against the Consent of their Parents; if the contract be (as they phrase it) in words of the present Tense."[5] Since these verbal distinctions are unintelligible to ordinary folk, it often happens, according to sixteenth-century moralists, that unsuspecting young people are lured into marriage by unscrupulous seducers. Thus Richard Whitforde inveighs against precontracts on the grounds that "many men when they cannot obtain their unclean desire of the woman will promise marriage"; but although he condemns the pleasures that follow such promises as "unlawful," Whitforde clearly regards the promises as binding.[6] Rabelais puts into the mouth of Pantagruel a fierce tirade against the marriage law and customs of the church, a tirade that fastens on the contrast between sober domesticity, prudently laying

up goods and the welfare and morals of children against the
future, and the sinister alliance of lechery and celibacy, alike
indifferent to the future of the world. Having spared no
expense in the "breeding and education" of their daughters,
hoping "by these commendable means . . . to bestow them
on the worthy sons of their well-deserving neighbors and
ancient friends," suitors themselves schooled "with the same
care and solicitude, to make them matches fit to attain to the
felicity of so happy marriage"—having in short invested their
hopes not only of earthly well-being but of a vicarious
immortality in their offspring, conscientious parents must
stand by helpless while their daughters are carried off and
seduced into marriage with the connivance of the church.
Such is the substance of Pantagruel's tirade. "By those wicked
laws and *mole-catching* customs, . . . there is no scurvy, mea-
sly, leprous, or pocky ruffian, pander, burn-marked, in his
own country, for his crimes and felonies, who may not vio-
lently snatch away and ravish what maid soever he had a
mind to pitch upon, how noble, how fair, how rich, honest
and chaste soever she be, and that out of the house of her
own father, in his own presence, from the bosom of her
mother, and in the sight and despite of her friends and kindred looking on so woful spectacle, provided that the rascally
villain be so cunning as to associate unto himself some *mysti-
cal flamen*, who, according to the covenant made betwixt
them two, shall be in hope some day to participate of the
prey. . . . May not these fathers and mothers (think you) be
sorrowful and heavy-hearted, when they see an unknown fellow, a vagabond, stranger, a barbarous lout, a rude cur, rotten,
fleshless, putrified, scraggy, boily, botchy, poor, a forlorn cai-
tiff and miserable snake, by an open rapt, snatch away before
their own eyes their so fair, delicate, neat, well-behavioured,
richly provided-for, and healthful daughters?"[7]

By the middle of the sixteenth century, opposition to "clandestine" marriages was strong enough throughout western Europe to force the Council of Trent to make a small concession to it, by stipulating for the first time that a priest had to witness the exchange of vows if a precontract was to be considered binding. About the same time a number of governments instituted measures designed to suppress clandestine marriages and to bring matrimonial affairs under the jurisdiction of the civil courts. A Dutch civil marriage law of 1580 required that marriages be publicized, registered, and performed in the presence of witnesses, persons under legal age signifying the consent of their parents.[8] In France a royal decree of 1556 allowed parents to disinherit children who married without their consent. This edict, however, exempted precontracts that had been followed by carnal union—an indication of the tenacity of the older idea that marriage consisted of an exchange of vows followed by cohabitation.[9]

In England the attack on clandestine marriage began in 1540, when Parliament passed a law (32 Henry VIII, c. 38) declaring that precontracts were not to be considered impediments to a later marriage unless followed by sexual intercourse. The preamble to this act condemned the canonical doctrine of precontracts on the grounds that it brought "many just marriages" into doubt, disinherited "lawful heirs," and contributed to general uncertainty regarding the status of marriage.[10] A few years later an act of Edward VI's reign repealed the section of the law concerning precontracts, ostensibly because it encouraged men and women to "break their own promises and faiths made by the one unto the other."[11] Other provisions of the act of 1540, notably those removing certain "impediments" to marriage, were restored by a law passed during the reign of Elizabeth, but although the Church of England repeatedly instructed curates to "exhort young folks to absteyne from privy contracts, and not to marry without the consent of such their parents and fryends as have auctority over them," the section on precontracts was not revived.[12] The canonical law of precontracts thus continued in force until the interregnum, when the Civil Marriage Act of 1653 transferred jurisdiction over marriage from the church courts, which had traditionally been empowered to enforce precontracts, to the justices of the peace. The same act required parental consent to all marriages in which one of the parties was under twenty-one and imposed heavy penalties for the abduction or fraudulent marriage of minors.

After the Restoration this law became void, and the evil of clandestine marriages allegedly continued to flourish unabated. Particularly scandalous were the so-called Fleet marriages, performed by clergymen sentenced to debtor's prison but confined to the Fleet district of London on parole. These disreputable curates evidently found it profitable, people said, to perform secret marriages in great number.[13] Their activities, together with the cynicism of the playwrights, the openness with which fashionable people married for money and titles, and the general looseness of morals in the period of the Restoration, gave rise to another outbreak of middle-class indignation, led once again by intellectuals eager to defend the sanctity of marriage in what they perceived to be an age of unparalleled depravity. "Nothing is a greater Mark of a degenerate and vitious Age," declared *The Spectator,* "than the common Ridicule which passes on" the married state— a condition that nevertheless "has in it all the Pleasures of Friendship, all the Enjoyments of Sense and Reason, and, indeed, all the Sweets of Life."[14] Addison and Steele spoke for a growing body of respectable opinion in upholding the value of marriage, in deploring the fashionable satires against it, and in condemning marriages that were based on greed, lust, or extravagant expectations "unfit for ordinary life."[15]

The defenders of matrimony were deeply offended by the treatment of marriage on the comic stage. The Restoration dramatists, following a long comic tradition, depicted marriage as an emotional absurdity, leading inevitably to quarrels, jealousy, and infidelity. Neither maidens nor wives, according to these conventions, were safe from the designs of the dedicated libertine, to whom in any case women usually offered no more than the most perfunctory resistance. "I look upon women," says a lecherous aristocrat in David Garrick's *The Clandestine Marriage*, "as the *ferae naturae*,—lawfull game—and every man who is qualified, has a natural right to pursue them."[16] In this play, first performed in 1766, the lecherous Lord Ogleby takes a much more understanding view of a secret marriage contracted by his kinsman Lovewell than the father of the bride, an avaricious London merchant. It is the latter who insists on the doctrine of parental consent. "You're not rich enough to think of a wife yet," he says to Lovewell. "A man of business should mind nothing but his business. . . . Get an estate, and a wife will follow of course" (Act I, scene 1).

If the Restoration playwrights are to be believed, cuckoldry lies in wait for every husband, no matter to what measures he resorts in order to prevent it. "A wife that has wit will out-wit her husband, and she that has no wit will be out-witted by others beside her husband, and so 'tis an equal lay, which makes the husband a Cuckold first and oftenest."[17] Merchants and tradesmen are especially apt to fall victim to this law. In the medieval stories that often furnish the plots of these cynical comedies, the lover is usually portrayed as a young man of no exalted station, and it is often the wife of

his lord that he seduces. The Restoration reverses the situation by turning the seducer into an aristocrat and his victims
into commoners. The Oedipal triangle disappears, and even
the theme of class aggression is uncertainly sustained, giving
way at times to a fantasy of unbridled and indiscriminate lust.
At such moments aristocratic satire against the middle classes
turns back on itself, condemning the profligacy of the age as
bitterly as the bourgeois satirists themselves. A lady's maid,
designated as an intermediary between her mistress and the
lady's lover, turns to the audience and delivers a caustic
speech, a speech that reeks of self-disgust.

> I would sooner choose to be some rich Ladies Woman,
> than many a poor Lords Wife. This Imployment was for-
> merly stil'd Bawding and Pimping—but our Age is more
> civiliz'd—and our Language much refin'd—it is now a
> modish piece of service only, and said, being complaisant,
> or doing a friend a kind office. Whore—(oh filthy broad
> word!) is now prettily call'd Mistress;—Pimp, Friend;
> Cuckold-maker, Gallant: thus the terms being civiliz'd the
> thing becomes more practicable,—what Clowns they were
> in former Ages.[18]

Eighteenth-century writers, it has often been noted, were
fascinated by the theme of seduction. Glorified on the comic
stage, the seducer was passionately condemned by the middle-class novelists, Defoe and Richardson in particular. Sometimes these writers view the problem of seduction, like their
sixteenth-century predecessors, through a father's eyes,
deploring the theft of a fortune; sometimes through the eyes
of injured innocence itself—a more direct, appealing, and
incidentally a more titillating perspective from which to view
the tragedy of seduction. Often these themes—the affront to

property and the affront to modesty—are intertwined, as they were on the marriage market itself, where virginity fetched a higher price than damaged goods. Hence the ambiguity of Pamela's resistance to her master: is she concerned to save her virtue or merely to enhance its value?

In his curious book *Conjugal Lewdness; or, Matrimonial Whoredom: A Treatise concerning the Use and Abuse of the Marriage Bed*—a book that stresses moderation, sobriety, delicacy, and mutual respect as the basis of married love—Defoe extols the statutes that have made "stealing of Ladies" a capital crime. In former times, he says, "it seemed a little hard, that a Gentleman might have the satisfaction of hanging a Thief that stole an old Horse from him, but could have no Justice against a Rogue for stealing his Daughter." Seduction became so common and the "Arts and Tricks" of "Brutes and Sharpers" refined to such a pitch that "it became almost dangerous for any one to leave a Fortune to the disposal of the Person that was to enjoy it, and where it was so left, the young lady went always in Danger of her Life, she was watch'd, laid in wait for, and, as it were, besieged by a continual Gang of Rogues, Cheats, Gamesters, and such like starving Crew." A single sentence here leads us from economics to sex, from the "fortune" to the poor girl herself, shut up like a prisoner in her room; if she ventured out of doors in those barbarous times, Defoe continues, "she was snatch'd up, seized upon, hurry'd up into a Coach and six, a Fellow dress'd up in a Clergyman's Habit to perform the Ceremony, and a Pistol clapt to her Breast to make her consent to be marry'd: And thus the Work was done."[19]

Just such a kidnapping falls to the lot of Harriet Byron, the heroine of Richardson's *Sir Charles Grandison*—except that in Harriet's case the villain is no starving sharper but a wealthy baronet, Sir Hargrave Pollexfen, who is attracted not to the girl's fortune but to her person. (Depending on whether the writer identifies himself with the father of the "bride" or more daringly, with the maiden herself, the seducer is perceived alternately as a fortune-hunter, usually of low birth, or as an unprincipled aristocrat, a libertine, a philosophical villain often equipped with advanced opinions on religious and moral questions.) Unwisely attending a masquerade dressed in a revealing and provocative gown of which she is foolishly vain, Harriet is "spirited away" in Sir Hargrave's coach. The lecherous villain has repeatedly begged Harriet to marry him, unlike the would-be seducers of Pamela and Clarissa, but although his female accomplices "seemed to believe," Harriet observes, "that marriage would make amends for every outrage," this reasoning makes no impression on a girl who insists on marrying only for love. Heedless of her wishes, Sir Hargrave takes Harriet to a house in the suburbs, where he confronts her with "the most horrible-looking clergyman that I ever beheld"—evidently a curate of the Fleet, ranging far afield in search of illicit fees, "his prayer-book opened, horrid sight! at the page of matrimony!" Harriet faints; Sir Hargrave sends away the parson in alarm and bundles her back into the carriage, from which she is later rescued by Sir Charles Grandison. Later still the odious Pollexfen repents, explaining that "he was resolved to strike a *bold stroke* for a wife, as were his words from the title of a play."[20]

In 1753 Parliament after heated debate passed an act "for the better preventing of clandestine marriages." The proponents of this legislation returned again and again to the dangers of seduction and "sham marriage," voicing arguments very similar to those of Defoe and Richardson. "How often," demanded the Attorney General, Sir Dudley Ryder, "have we known the heir of a good family seduced, and engaged in a clandestine marriage, perhaps with a common strumpet? How often have we known a rich heiress carried off by a man of low birth, or perhaps by an infamous sharper?"[21] Lord Barrington hoped that the new law would help to protect women from "sham marriage."[22] John Bond professed to find it astonishing that anyone should oppose such an eminently sensible measure. The question before the country, he said, was simply "whether we shall leave our young gentlemen of fortune, whilst under age, a prey to bawds and prostitutes, and our young ladies of fortune, whilst under age, a prey to sharpers and fortune-hunters." The plight of the "young lady of fortune . . . seduced by a sharper or footman" was sufficiently obvious, he should have thought, to command immediate and sympathetic attention.[23] Lord Chancellor Hardwicke, the chief architect of the Marriage Act, likewise professed amazement to hear the measure opposed. "It would not, indeed, have been surprising, that young men in the warmth of their constitution, should be averse to any regulations, which seemed to interfere with their passions and sanguine pursuits: but it was very extraordinary to see grave and solemn persons turn a law so necessary for the public good into an engine of dark intrigue and faction, and into an occasion of forming a party, and trying its strength."[24]

Opponents of the Hardwicke bill saw it as an aristocratic plot to "secure all the rich heiresses in the kingdom." Wealth, they argued—"the blood of the body politic," as one of them put it—must circulate freely, and to this end marriage must be based not on calculation but on love and sexual attraction.

When a young commoner makes his addresses to a rich heiress [said Robert Nugent], he has no friend but his superior merit, and that little deity called love, whose influence over a young lady always decreases as she increases in years; for by the time she comes of age, pride and ambition seizes [sic] possession of her breast likewise, and banishes from thence the little deity called love, or if he preserves a corner from his friend, it is only to introduce him as a gallant, not a husband. Therefore I may prophesy, that if this Bill passes into a law, no commoner will ever marry a rich heiress, unless his father be a minister of state, nor will a peer's eldest son marry the daughter of a commoner, unless she be a rich heiress.[25]

"Nugent took [the bill] to pieces severely and sensibly," wrote Horace Walpole, "and pointed out the impropriety of it in a commercial nation, and the ill-nature and partiality of the restrictions." "It was amazing," Walpole reflected, "in a country where liberty gives choice, where trade and money confer equality, and where facility of marriage had always been supposed to produce populousness,—it was amazing to see a law promulgated, that cramped inclination, that discountenanced matrimony, and that seemed to annex as sacred privileges to birth, as could be devised in the proudest, poorest little Italian principality. . . ."[26]

Because they condemned the aristocratic tendencies they saw in the bill, denounced marriages of interest and the adulterous intrigues to which they allegedly gave rise, and defended love as the most secure basis of marriage, it is tempting to see the opponents of the Marriage Act as advocates of a distinctively modern concept of marriage, spokesmen of a progressive middle class against aristocrats who looked on marriage merely as a means of arranging alliances between great families and of preserving a noble lineage. The conflict over the Marriage Act might be seen, in other words, as another chapter in the struggle for individual rights—in this case, the right of free choice in marriage. In a number of respects, however, the opponents of the Hardwicke bill were proposing a very old-fashioned conception of marriage, one that stressed the element of sexual attraction at a time when leaders of respectable opinion were more and more united in emphasizing the importance of prudence and foresight, the need for parental consent, and the desirability of postponing marriage until the folly of youth was safely past. Lord Barrington would have gone so far as to forbid all marriages of people under twenty-one, men and women alike.[27] The opponents of the Marriage Act, on the other hand, condemned anything that would delay the age of marriage—for "the flower of youth," as Charles Townshend noted, "the highest bloom of a woman's beauty, is from sixteen to twenty-one: it is then that a young woman of little or no fortune has the best chance for disposing of herself to advantage in marriage; shall we make it impossible for her to do so, without the consent of an indigent and mercenary father?"[28] To the legislators on the other side of the marriage question, this harping on a young girl's beauty must have appeared a little unseemly—what did beauty have to do, after all, with the weighty topic at hand? Their ideal of marriage was of "a sedate and fixed love," in the words of the Earl of Hillsborough, not "a sudden flash of passion which dazzles the understanding, but is in a moment extinguished."[29]

The issues underlying the controversy touched off by the Marriage Act emerged most sharply in debates about its probable effect on the poor. One of the most important objections to the bill, an objection that figured prominently in all the speeches against it, was that the provisions requiring strict publicity and registration would discourage common people from marrying. For one thing, it was said, the measure flew in the face of a strong popular prejudice against publication of banns. This aversion, in fact, had caused the evil of Fleet marriages to arise in the first place. "If the parson of every parish had a power to marry people at his church without either license or proclamation of banns, I believe, we should never have any such marriage shop set up as that at Keith's chapel." Such was the contention of Colonel George Haldane, who went on to argue, accordingly, that the immediate evil—the irregular Fleet marriages, which had brought "private" marriages in general into discredit—could be remedied by the simple expedient of doing away with banns and licenses altogether.[30]

Not only did public marriages offend modesty, they were expensive; this too, in the view of several speakers, explained the attraction of the Fleet. So-called clandestine marriage, according to Colonel Haldane, arose from putting too many obstacles in the way of marriage itself. "If a marriage could be solemnized as conveniently and for as little expence, at the parish church, and by a regular clergyman, even the most vulgar would chuse to be married there."[31]

Besides enforcing publicity, the Hardwicke Act deprived the ecclesiastical courts of the power to enforce precontracts—this was its most important provision. According to opponents of the bill, this reform would fall like a blight on lower-class marriage. On this point the arguments of Robert Nugent are worth pursuing in some detail; not only do they shed light on popular marriage customs, but they illustrate more clearly than any other arguments the animus of the opposition to the Marriage Act.

The common man, according to Nugent, does not deliberate before marrying. "Would a poor labouring man, who can by hard labour, earn but a little more than is necessary for supporting himself in what he may think an elegant manner:

would such a man, I say, incumber himself with a wife and child, if he were directed by nothing but the dictates of wisdom and foresight?" Only "an ungovernable and irresistible passion" leads people to propagate.

> In the country where I sometimes reside [Nugent continued], I have the honour to be a justice of the peace. . . . Of course I have had several country wenches brought before me by the parish officers for being with child: she names the father, generally some young country fellow in the neighbourhood: he is immediately sent for, and confesses his being the father: the consequence is, he must either agree to marry her, or go to Bridewell: if he agrees to the first, I send them directly to church, and they are presently married.

But if it takes a month or more to arrange the ceremony, as will be the case under the proposed legislation, the young man is certain to run off, leaving "both the girl and the parish in the lurch."

"Another case often happens," Nugent continues: a young man impregnates his fiancée and marries her privately to save her honor, "so that none of the neighbors shall know but that they were married before the child was begot." The new law prevents such marriages, both by requiring publicity and by depriving precontracts of their binding force.

> A young woman is but too apt by nature to trust to the honour of the man she loves, and to admit him to her bed upon a solemn promise to marry her. Surely the moral obligation is as binding as if they had been actually married: but you are by this Bill to declare it null and void, even though in writing.

The Hardwicke bill, according to Nugent, was only one of several measures designed to prevent the poor from marrying and from reproducing themselves.

> The humour of preventing the poor from marrying prevails too much of late in all parts of this country: our numerous Bills for inclosing commons have a great tendency this way, and those wise parish politicians, called parish-officers, are every where destroying cottages, because they encourage the poor to marry and beget children, which may become burthensome to the parish. Do these wiseheads think, that labourers, servants, common seamen and soldiers are not necessary for the support and security of this kingdom?[32]

It should be noted that Nugent was not alone in seeing the Hardwicke bill as part of an aristocratic conspiracy against the common people. The bill was "only a prelude," according to Charles Townshend, to another bill "restoring the old law of intails."

The eighteenth century was in many ways a period of aristocratic revival in England, and these suspicions of aristocratic influence were not unfounded. But it is important to understand that the resurgence of aristocratic power was based on an agrarian revolution that was eradicating feudal traditions, abolishing feudal tenures, and commercializing agriculture, in the course of which the landed gentry and even the nobility had to acquire a thoroughly "middle-class" outlook on the management of their estates, on child-raising and education, and on marriage. Lawrence Stone has shown that as early as the first part of the seventeenth century, "the concept of an inward-turned, isolated, conjugal family, already familiar to the *bourgeoisie*, was well on the way to acceptance among the aristocracy."[33] One of the best indications of this tendency is the steadily rising age of aristocratic marriage, especially for women. During the course of the eighteenth century the mean age of first marriage for women of the peerage rose from 22.2 to 24.[34] A French observer attributed the lateness of marriage in the British aristocracy to the closeness of the marital tie, the high esteem in which marriage was held. "Husband and wife are always together and share the same society." Since a bad marriage, he thought, "must make life a misery" in England, courtship tended to be prolonged. "An Englishman . . . makes a greater effort to get to know his bride before marriage; she has the same desire and I believe that is why marriage before the age of twenty-five or twenty-eight is rare." Another reason was that "it is usual to set up house immediately after marriage. The young couple never stay with thir parents."[35]

When marriage is late and courtship prolonged, young couples are in a strong position to resist matches arranged by their parents. It should not surprise us, therefore, that arranged marriage in England had for some time been under attack; presumably this attack reflected, as well as contributing to, a change in aristocratic courtship patterns that had been in process ever since the sixteenth century. As we have already seen, condemnation of "forced marriage" is by no means incompatible with an insistence on the need for parental consent. These attitudes have a common source in the concept of marriage as a lifelong union based on compatibility. Once the element of companionship in marriage came to be emphasized, as a consequence of humanist and Protestant thought, marriages of interest and marriages of impulse both tended to be rejected, at least in theory, by the middle class and even by the aristocracy. Parents who forced marriage on young people obviously unsuited to each other were to be condemned; but so were couples who rushed into marriages based on nothing more solid than a momentary infatuation. Hence the insistence on parental consent and, more generally, on the importance of postponing marriage until the participants were capable of arriving at a mature decision.

It was precisely passion, however, that the opponents of the Marriage Act saw as the necessary basis of marriage, especially among the poor. To be sure, they too spoke of the need for love, but their insistence on the desirability of early marriages shows that they conceived of love as a function of sexual attraction rather than a product of mature deliberation and long acquaintance.[36] When they defined the essence of marriage as an exchange of vows followed by cohabitation, questioned the need for publicity, and emphasized the force of sexual attraction, men like Nugent, Haldane, and Townshend were speaking for an older tradition, rooted in popular practice—a tradition that had been under increasing criticism, culminating in the agitation for the Marriage Act.

That agitation had two objects—to protect the children of the middle and upper classes from rash marriages and from the danger of seduction, which obsessed respectable opinion in the eighteenth century, and on the other hand to impose the new "middle-class" ideals on the rest of the population. As the opponents of the bill correctly discerned, this latter attempt was part of a more general movement to discipline the lower orders—by passing stringent laws against vagrancy and idleness, by building workhouses and "hospitals" to segregate deviants and/or put them to work, by enclosing the common lands and attacking the traditional rights of cottagers, by putting an end to many of the traditional rights of domestic servants, and finally by discouraging marriage among the poor, partly on the grounds that population was growing faster than the nation's resources. The Marriage Act of 1753 should be viewed as among other things another dose of what R. H. Tawney called "the new medicine for poverty."[37] It was one of a whole series of measures by means of which eighteenth-century reformers attempted to bring about "a general reformation of manners among the lower sort of people."[38]

On the one hand, respectable folk were withdrawing from the promiscuous society of an earlier time into the privacy of their drawing rooms, in houses increasingly set off from working-class neighborhoods and from the working life of the city.[39] On the other hand, they insisted that the lower orders live up to the new standards of industry, punctuality, thrift, and "rational" domestic comfort. It was in the eighteenth century that masters gradually retired from the company of their servants, now segregated "below stairs," converted many of the customary perquisites of domestic service into contractual arrangements, and abolished the tradition of vails—tips given to servants by guests of the house—on the grounds that it "wounded the authority of masters," encouraged insubordination, and degraded hospitality by turning the private house into a kind of hotel, where guests "are obliged to pay their reckoning before they go away."[40] It was in the eighteenth century also that reformers mounted a systematic attack on the traditional games and pastimes of the people. Fairs and football, they argued, bull-baiting and cock-fighting and boxing were cruel and inhumane, and moreover they blocked up public thoroughfares, disrupted the daily routine of business, distracted the people from their work, encouraged habits of idleness, extravagance, and insubordination, and gave rise to licentiousness and debauchery. In the name of "rational enjoyment" and the spirit of "improvement," the laboring man was urged to forsake his riotous public sports and "wakes" and to stay at his hearth, in the respectable comfort of the domestic circle. When exhortation failed, the reformers resorted to political action. They were opposed by a conservative coalition that crossed class lines, the commoners having been joined in the defense of their "immemorial" enjoyments by traditionalists among the gentry, especially the rural gentry not yet infected with evangelical piety, sentimental humanitarianism, and the dogma of enterprise and progress. "What would be the Consequence," they asked, "if all such Diversions were entirely banished? The common People seeing themselves cut off from all Hope of this Enjoyment, would become dull and spiritless . . . : And not only so, but thro' the absolute Necessity of diverting themselves at Times, they would addict themselves rather to less warrantable Pleasures."[41] Exactly the same spirit animated the opposition to the Marriage Act. Here too the upper classes were divided against themselves, one side deeply critical of popular customs, desirous also of protecting the children of respectable families from impetuous marriages with servants and "sharpers"—the other side defending traditional practices on the grounds that their suppression might lead to something worse.

That the Hardwicke Act, with its stringent provisions against clandestine marriage and precontracts, was passed by a solid majority (though with many amendments and modifications of its original provisions), shows that the "middle-class" view of marriage now commanded a good deal of support in the English aristocracy and gentry as well as in the middle class itself. On the other hand, the extent and vigor of the opposition, not only in Parliament but in the country as a whole, suggest the tenacity of the traditions the Marriage Act was intended to extinguish. In spite of the concerted attack on them, those traditions survived—to what extent cannot be easily ascertained. The great increase both in illegitimate births and in bridal pregnancies, in the second half of the eighteenth century, sheds some light, if only indirectly, on changes in courtship and marriage patterns.

During the debates on the Marriage Act, opponents of the measure predicted that if the violent passions of youth were denied the legitimate outlet of marriage, they would inevitably seek other outlets. The natural consequence of the law would therefore be an enormous increase in bastardy and sexual license of all kinds.[42] The ratio of illegitimate to legitimate births did indeed rise very sharply in the second half of the eighteenth century.[43] The fact that this rise occurred all over Europe, and also in America, shows that it can hardly be attributed to a single piece of legislation (any more than it can be attributed to that all-purpose explanation, the "industrial revolution"). The most plausible explanation of the dramatic increase in illegitimacy is that it reflected the dislocations, the demoralization, and the collapse of family discipline that accompanied the proletarianization of lower-class life. The rise in the proportion of women who bore more than one bastard suggests the growth of a class of people among whom irregular sexual activities had become habitual; it may also indicate an increase in prostitution.[44]

To what extent the rise in illegitimacy reflected a general shift in sexual attitudes and practices is a matter of dispute. Edward Shorter argues that the rise in illegitimacy reflected, among other things, a shift from "instrumental" to "expressive" sexuality. Peter Laslett and Karla Oosterveen, on the other hand, believe that fluctuations in illegitimacy do not even necessarily reflect changes in the prevalence of sexual intercourse outside marriage, let alone a change in attitudes. But there is reason to believe that older courtship patterns, whereby betrothals had the force of marriage itself and were often followed by intercourse, were breaking down long before the Marriage Act officially condemned them. Robert

Nugent, it will be recalled, attributed many clandestine marriages to the fear that neighbors would learn of the bride's pregnancy. This remark may reflect a middle-class misunderstanding of a popular practice; on the other hand, it may indicate that premarital intercourse, long condemned by middle-class moralists like Defoe, was coming to be regarded as shameful by the common people themselves, even when it was sanctioned by the intention to marry. This in turn would indicate that betrothal was losing its binding character, in custom as well as in law. The older practices presumably presupposed a fairly stable social setting, in which betrothals were usually a matter of general knowledge. The disruption of village life, the enclosure of common lands, and the growth of a rootless and highly mobile class of laborers, paupers, and vagrants must have greatly increased the amount of casual sexual activity outside marriage and the likelihood that it would lead to the birth of bastards rather than to marriage.

The fact that the level of bridal pregnancy rose simultaneously with the level of illegitimacy does not necessarily invalidate this hypothesis.[45] Bridal pregnancies are of two types—those resulting from cohabitation between persons planning to marry (even if the decision to marry is made only after the woman becomes pregnant), and those resulting from casual sexual contacts between men and women who by no stretch of the imagination can be said to be "courting." The second type, as Peter Laslett has noted, is "very close to bastardy," even though children born of such unions are registered as legitimate. What proportion of the eighteenth-century increase in bridal pregnancy was accounted for by these irregular unions? It is obviously difficult to be sure. The most important evidence would seem to be the bride's age at marriage. If most women marry in their middle twenties, as they did in England in the eighteenth century, pregnant brides who marry in their teens or even in their early twenties might be presumed to have become pregnant in the course of casual and irregular encounters to which marriage was a desperate afterthought. (Otherwise we should have to assume, what is most unlikely, that couples having sexual relations in their late teens, say, normally expected to be "courting" for another five or six years.) If the age of marriage among pregnant brides in the second half of the eighteenth century was falling, therefore, it could persuasively be argued that irregular encounters were becoming more frequent—increasing, that is, in proportion to those sanctioned by an intention to marry. Unfortunately I have seen no evidence that bears on this question, one way or the other.

It is generally assumed that the "modernization" of marriage brings increasing freedom of choice to the young, as arranged marriages give way to marriages based on love. If that is the case, then the beginnings of "modernization" in England, and for that matter in most of western Europe, must be dated from the sixteenth century. From that time on, and perhaps from a much earlier time, marriages in England took place at a remarkably late age, and the proportion of those who never married at all, moreover, was much higher than it was in other parts of the world. These two facts indicate that marriage rested on the free consent of the individuals to a much greater degree than is the case under systems where marriages are almost universally arranged and where marriage, accordingly, occurs early and is almost universal.

Yet this very freedom came under increasing attack at precisely the moment when the "modern" conception of marriage began to take shape. In its early stages modernization took the form of an attack on "forced marriage," to be sure, but it also took the form of a new insistence on the importance of parental consent, on the need for prudence and caution—and also, it should be noted, on the indissolubility of the marital bond. Specifically it took the form of a protracted struggle against precontracts and "clandestine" marriage—part of a general campaign, on the part of bourgeois reformers, to impose new standards of personal morality and new patterns of work discipline, and to inculcate the virtues of thrift, denial of immediate gratifications, and foresight in a population that stubbornly clung to older conventions.

NOTES

1. Quoted in Steven Marcus, *The Other Victorians* (New York, 1966), p. 146 n.

2. The classical canonical doctrine on spousals and marriage was formulated by Gratian (359–383). According to him, a valid marriage rests on (1) physical union accompanied by (2) a declaration of intent to live as man and wife. Later canonists, following Peter Lombard and Alexander III, distinguished two forms of these declarations, one in which the promises were exchanged in words of the present tense, the other in which the future tense was used. Under this new doctrine spousals *de praesenti* were valid and binding whether or not they were followed by physical union, while carnal knowledge was required, on the other hand, in order to validate spousals *de futuro*. (The doctrine of "presumptive marriage," a further refinement, held that cohabitation was legal ground for assuming the foregoing promises—spousals *de futuro*—to have been made.) George Elliott Howard, *A History of Matrimonial Institutions* (Chicago, 1904), I, 334–08; Chilton Latham Powell, *English Domestic Relations, 1487–1653* (New York, 1917), pp. 1–13.

It is important not to make too much of the distinction between spousals *de praesenti* and spousals *de futuro*. A learned commentator in the seventeenth century admirably expresses the sense of the canon law on this point: "Since it is the very Consent of Mind only which maketh Matrimony, we are to regard not their Words, but their Intents, not the formality of the Phrase, but the drift of their Determination, not the outward sound of their Lips, which cannot speak more cunningly, but the inward Harmony or Agreement of their Hearts, which mean uprightly. . . . Where two intend to contract spousals *de praesenti*, there is Matrimony always contracted, although the words import but future Consent only." Henry Swinburne, *Of Spousals* (London, 1686), quoted in Howard, *Matrimonial Institutions,* I, 342–43.

Luther gives the same interpretation of the canon law. "The lawyers and canonists are of opinion, that the substance of matrimony is the consent of the bride and bridegroom, and that the privilege and power of the parents is [*sic*] but an accidental thing. . . . Consent is the substance and ground of matrimony." *The Table Talk of Martin Luther,* William Hazlitt, ed. and trans. (London, 1857), p. 305.

3. Book III, ch. 48 (Urquhart translation).

4. "Do you first endeavour to know your own Mind thoroughly, and don't be govern'd by your Passion, but by Reason. The Passion of Love is but temporary; but what proceeds from Reason is lasting." "A Lover and a Maiden," *The Colloquies of Erasmus,* N. Bailey, trans. (London, 1878), I, 223.

5. Ibid.; "The Virgin Averse to Matrimony," I, 235. See also the exchange in "The Old Men's Dialogue" (I, 347): "Was she your Wife?" "There had past some Words between us in the future Tense, but there had been carnal Copulation in the present Tense." "How could you leave her then?"

6. Because "hot love is soon cold," one of the partners may choose to "deny the contract and so unlawfully . . . marry otherwise and live in adultery all their lifetime." For this reason "it is a great jeopardy to make any such contract without records which must be two at least." Richard Whitforde, *A Werke for Householders* (London, 1530).

7. Book III, ch. 48. See also M. A. Screech, *The Rabelaisian Marriage: Aspects of Rabelais's Religion, Ethics, and Comic Philosophy* (London, 1958), pp. 45–48.

8. Howard, *Matrimonial Institutions,* I, 409.

9. David Hunt, *Parents and Children in History: The Psychology of Family Life in Early Modern France* (New York, 1970), pp. 60–61. "The deeply ingrained idea that marriage was based on the freely given consent of the bride and groom," Hunt observes, "was not to be eradicated by the arguments of a handful of legists." It does not necessarily follow, however, that "in spite of the opposition of parents and legists," in Hunt's words, " 'love' played a considerable part in the formation of marriage bonds by the seventeenth century" (pp. 65, 78–79).

10. John Cordy Jeaffreson, *Brides and Bridals* (London, 1872), I, 126, 114 n.

11. 2 and 3 Edward VI c. 23, quoted in ibid, I, 124 n.

12. Jeaffreson, *Brides and Bridals*, I, 82 n. See also Louis B. Wright, *Middle-Class Culture in Elizabethan England* (Ithaca, 1935), pp. 208–09.

13. Howard, *Matrimonial Institutions*, I, 440–42; Jeaffreson, *Brides and Bridals*, I, 122–66.

14. No. 261, December 29, 1711.

15. No. 479, September 8, 1712.

16. Act IV, scene 2; Cecil A. Moore, ed., *Twelve Famous Plays of the Restoration and Eighteenth Century* (New York, 1933), p. 707.

17. Edward Ravenscroft, *The London Cuckolds*, Act I, scene 1 (Montague Summers, ed., *Restoration Comedies* [Boston, 1922]), p. 151.

18. *The London Cuckolds*, Act III, scene 1 (ibid., pp. 190–1). On the *fabliaux*, see the authoritative study by Joseph Bédier, *Les Fabliaux* (Paris, 1925).

19. Daniel Defoe, *Conjugal Lewdness* [1727] (Gainesville, Fla., 1967), pp. 366–67.

20. Samuel Richardson, *The History of Sir Charles Grandison*, letters 29–35 (Oxford, 1936), I, 227–64.

21. William Cobbett, ed., *The Parliamentary History of England* (London, 1813), XV, 3. See also debates on the Marriage Act in *Gentleman's Magazine*, XXIII (1753), 399–400, 452, 538; XXIV (1754), 145; XXV (1755), 212.

22. Ibid., XV, 27. Cobbett, *Parliamentary History*, XV, 27.

23. Ibid., XV, 41, 48.

24. Ibid., XV, 85 n.

25. Ibid., XV, 14–15.

26. Horace Walpole, *Memoirs of the Reign of King George the Second* (London, 1847), I, 337–38, 340.

27. Cobbett, *Parliamentary History*, XV, 28.

28. Ibid., XV, 59.

29. Ibid., XV, 63.

30. Ibid., XV, 40. Several speakers alluded to the popular resistance to publication of banns. In this connection it is interesting to learn that

according to a folk tradition common both in England and in France, children born to a woman who heard her own banns read out in church would be deaf and dumb. Christina Hole, *English Folklore* (London, 1940), p. 18; Jeaffreson, *Brides and Bridals*, I, 133; Arnold Van Gennep, *Manuel de Folklore Français Contemporain* (Paris, 1943), I, 290–91.

31. Cobbett, *Parliamentary History*, XV, 41.

32. Ibid., XV, 17–22.

33. Lawrence Stone, *The Crisis of the Aristocracy* (Oxford, 1965), p. 669.

34. T. H. Hollingsworth, "A Demographic Study of the British Ducal Families," in D. V. Glass and D. E. C. Eversley, *Population in History* (London, 1965), p. 365.

35. François de la Rochefoucauld, quoted in J. Hajnal, "European Marriage Patterns in Perspective," ibid., p. 115.

36. The reader should not infer from their advocacy of early marriage that early marriage was in fact common. This view was formerly very prevalent; see Frederick J. Furnivall, *Child-Marriages, Divorces, and Ratifications in the Diocese of Chester, 1561–6* (London, 1897), a book that Howard believed documented "the astonishing prevalence of child-marriages" in earlier times (*Matrimonial Institutions*, I, 400). The widespread impression that most people in early modern Europe married very young has now been shown to be erroneous. See Peter Laslett, *The World We Have Lost* (New York, 1965), ch. 4; J. Hajnal, "European Marriage Patterns in Perspective," Louis Lenry, "The Population of France in the Eighteenth Century," and P. Deprez, "The Demographic Development of Flanders in the Eighteenth Century," all in Glass and Eversley, *Population in History*, pp. 101–43, 454–55, 614–15. In general the age of marriage was lower in the aristocracy, a fact that may help to account for the impression that everybody married early. In France the average age at first marriage in the peerage fell from 25.5 to 21.3 for men and from 20 to 18.4 for women over the period from 1650 to 1799. "On this point," says Henry, "there is as much difference between the top of the social scale and the mass of the population as between two populations of different cultures, such as Mohammedans and Europeans." In England, however, the rise in the average age of marriage in the aristocracy was narrowing the gap between aristocratic marriage patterns and those of the rest of the country.

37. *Religion and the Rise of Capitalism*, ch. 4.

38. London *Packet*, No. 807, December 21–23, 1774, quoted in J. Jean Hecht, *The Domestic Servant Class in Eighteenth-Century England* (London, 1956), p. 173.

39. See Philippe Ariès, *Centuries of Childhood*, Robert Baldick, trans. (New York, 1962), pp. 414–15 and passim.

40. Quoted in Hecht, *Domestic Servant Class*, pp. 160–61.

41. Robert W. Malcolmson, *Popular Recreations in English Society, 1700–1850* (Cambridge, 1973), p. 70.

42. Cobbett, *Parliamentary History*, XV, 20, 60, 70.

43. Edward Shorter, "Illegitimacy, Sexual Revolution, and Social Change in Modern Europe," in Theodore B. Rabb and Robert I. Rothberg, eds., *The Family in History* (New York, 1973), pp. 48–84; Peter Laslett and Karla Oosterveen, "Long-Term Trends in Bastardy in England," *Population Studies*, XXVII (1973), 255–84.

44. Ibid. Shorter, however, thinks that there is no correlation between prostitution and illegitimacy or, if anything, that there is a negative correlation; Rabb and Rothberg, *The Family in History*, p. 63.

45. Laslett and Oosterveen, op. cit., pp. 269–70; P. H. E. Hair, "Bridal Pregnancy in Rural England in Earlier Centuries," *Population Studies*, XX (1966), 233–43, and "Bridal Pregnancy in Earlier Rural England Further Examined," ibid., XXIV (1970), 59–70.

4

Bourgeois Domesticity, the Revolt against Patriarchy, and the Attack on Fashion

The nineteenth-century cult of domesticity, so called, originated in a systematic attack on patriarchal authority, led by an international elite of doctors, philanthropists, and humanitarians. These worthies had to wage a war on two fronts, against aristocratic license on the one hand and against popular immorality and sedition on the other. Hannah More, one of the first to advocate a general Christianization of society as the best antidote to political disorder, simultaneously criticized the manners of the "great and the gay" and sought to disseminate Christian principles among the poor. Known today chiefly as an exponent of a sickly, unbearably sentimental form of piety, More was a sharp-eyed observer of an important shift in middle-class manners, which she sought to expose and reverse. By the end of the eighteenth century the middle class in England no longer consisted mainly of farmers, artisans, and small tradesmen. Upwardly mobile merchants and entrepreneurs aped aristocratic ways; their wives no longer managed dairies or worked with their husbands behind counters but sought to transform themselves into ladies, creatures of fashion. As early as 1697 Daniel Defoe detected the beginnings of this trend in his *Essay on Projects.* Middle-class women, he said, acted "as if they were ashamed of being tradesmen's wives"; they did not like "to be seen in the counting house." Addison and Steele, writing in the same vein, deplored the effects of a fashionable education. "To make her an agreeable person is the main purpose of her parents; . . . to that all their care [is] directed, and from this general folly of parents we owe all our present numerous race of coquettes."[1]

If we can believe Hannah More, the "contagion of dissipated manners" had become almost irresistible in her time. In 1799, in a set of *Strictures . . . with a View to the Principles and Conduct among Women of Rank and Fortune,* she complained that "the showy education of women tends chiefly to qualify them for the glare of public assemblies"—balls and dinners "en masse," which served as the stage on which young women displayed their charms before an audience of prospective suitors. Girls were increasingly brought up "with a view to the greater probability of their being splendidly married," according to More. Once this aim was achieved, however, they found it difficult to renounce the habit of flirtation. The husband who chose a wife as he would choose a picture at a gallery found, to his dismay, that she "will not, . . . when brought home, stick so quietly to the spot where he fixes her, but will escape to the exhibition-room again, and continue to be displayed at every subsequent exhibition." Bored, flirtatious wives, More believed, set the prevailing tone of fashionable dissipation and worldly cynicism. "That cold compound of irony, irreligion, selfishness, and sneer, which the French call *persiflage*, has of late years made an incredible progress in blasting the opening buds of piety in young persons of fashion. A cold pleasantry, a temporary cant words, the jargon of the day . . . blight the first promise of seriousness." Since the "general state of civil society" depended on the "estimation in which they are held," women wielded enormous influence for better or worse. Unfortunately the "frenzy of accomplishments" was "no longer restricted within the usual limits of rank and fortune." The "middle orders" had "caught the contagion." "It rages downward," unfitting ordinary people for the "active duties of their own very important condition." Formerly it was said that "most worth and virtue are to be found in the middle station," but the spread of "frigid sarcasm," "habitual levity," "indolent selfishness," and affected "extravagance of expression" threatened to render that saying "obsolete."

Women should seek to make themselves useful, More thought, not ornamental. They should submit to "dry, tough reading" instead of wasting time on novels. "Serious study" would counter the "frivolous turn of female conversation and the petty nature of female employments." Women should study difficult subjects like history and geography. If it was objected that they were incapable of intellectual exertion, More replied that no one knew what women could do until they were given the chance to prove themselves. Even under the unfavorable conditions that obtained, many women were "nobly rising from all the pressure of a disadvantageous education, . . . and exhibiting the most unambiguous marks of a vigorous understanding, a correct judgment, and a sterling piety."

Much of this was quite consonant with a feminist point of view, although More did not regard herself as a feminist and went out of her way, in fact, to disparage the leading feminist among her contemporaries, Mary Wollstonecraft. Because Wollstonecraft's work had nevertheless made a deep impression on her, and because she found it difficult to formulate a compelling reply, it is important to understand the reasons behind More's rejection of feminism. She associated it with the *"précieuses ridicules,"* seventeenth-century women of letters who pressed the case for sexual equality—or rather, for the superiority of women—from their privileged position in aristocratic salons and "with more warmth than wisdom." The literary controversy about women, which produced "so many volumes, and so little wit," grew out of the revival of learning in the Renaissance, according to More. "The novelty of that knowledge that was then bursting out from the dawn of a long dark night kindled all the ardours of a feminine mind, and the ladies fought zealously for a portion of that renown which the reputation of learning was beginning to bestow." Even though their ambitions unfortunately outran their abilities, their social position made it possible for these women to attract chivalrous "champions" from the ranks of men dependent on their favor—"parasites who offered . . . homage to female genius," just as knights had once paid homage to female beauty. Seventeenth-century feminism flourished in a courtly milieu, and it was this aristocratic background, I suspect—which prompted the belief that the *querelle des femmes* was nothing more than a new kind of gallantry—that offended More's thoroughly middle-class sensibility.

Not that her reservations did not extend to the middle-class feminism of Mary Wollstonecraft. "The contest [between men and women] has recently been revived with added fury," she observed, but "whereas the ancient demand was merely . . . a shadowy claim to a few unreal acres of Parnassian territory, the revived contention has taken a more serious turn, and brings forward political as well as intellectual pretensions. . . . The imposing term of rights has been produced to sanctify the claims of our female pretenders." Because the new feminism was "more serious" than the old, it was more difficult to counter. More's reply rested on the misrepresentation that feminists proposed to abolish the distinction between men and women, that they ignored the mutual dependence of men and women and set them at odds with each other, and that they were consumed with a "feverish thirst for a fame as unattainable as inappropriate." Latter-day feminists, More objected unconvincingly, were traitors to the "delicacy of their female character." Her defensive tone betrayed a want of confidence in such arguments. "Is the author then undervaluing her own sex?—No. It is her zeal for their true interests which leads her to oppose their imaginary rights."

The reason More found Wollstonecraft's brand of feminism so difficult to refute is that the two women shared a great deal of common ground. More was put off not so much by the ideas advanced in *The Vindication of the Rights of Woman* as by Wollstonecraft's personal history: her scandalous affair with Gilbert Imlay, her suicide attempts, her unconventional marriage to the notorious anarchist and freethinker William Godwin. Godwin's memoir of his wife, written shortly after her death in childbirth, did her a disservice by dwelling on her disappointments in love at the expense of her writings. But when the *Vindication* appeared in 1791, ten years earlier, the initial response was surprisingly favorable, on the whole; "most reviewers," according to R. M. James, "took it to be a sensible treatise on female education." Like Hannah More, Wollstonecraft advocated an education that would make women useful rather than ornamental. Like More, she deplored the worldly cynicism prevalent in fashionable circles. Both women objected to the premature exposure of young people to the ways of the world, at an age when such knowledge could only make them affected, snobbish, and insincere. Some of the most vigorous writing in the *Vindication* sought to show how a worldly-wise education, of the type advocated by Lord Chesterfield and his imitators, dampened the "ardor of youth" and crippled the "luxuriancy of fancy." "An unwelcome knowledge of life," Wollstonecraft wrote, "produces almost a satiety of life." Unless knowledge was acquired in the course of experience appropriate to its season, it merely hardened the heart. But since experience entailed "labor and sorrow," adults tried to spare their children by warning them of disappointments ahead, only to find that they had inadvertently condemned them to something worse than disappointment—a "mean opinion of human nature" in a world without wonder.

Like Hannah More, Wollstonecraft sought to recall the middle orders to a proper understanding of themselves. The "middle rank," she thought, was the one in which "talents thrive best." Unable to enjoy the admiration gratuitously bestowed on wealth and beauty, the middle class had to rely on its "virtues and abilities." Now that the middle class was becoming wealthy in its own right, however, it was beginning to adopt standards foreign to itself. Women, in particular, were flattered by the attention they attracted as "fine sentimental ladies." A new breed of women, "unfit to manage a family" or to raise children, lived exclusively for love and sexual intrigue. Sense had given way to sensibility. "Trifling employments have made woman a trifler." Wholly dependent on their husbands for support, middle-class women now found themselves in the position of aristocratic classes as a whole, which reconciled themselves to an idle, unproductive, parasitic life on the grounds that elegance, not virtue, was the supreme end of existence.

Wollstonecraft reserved her sharpest invective for the aristocratic code of love, which made women either slaves or tyrants, never the equals of men. Lacking economic independence, women sought to gain power over men by exploiting the "sensual homage paid to beauty." By "degrading themselves" in this way, they achieved an "illegitimate power," a "short-lived tyranny" at the expense of self-respect. They ruled by "cunning" and sexual attraction—by "infantine airs that undermine esteem even whilst they excite desire." Rousseau's *Émile*, as Wollstonecraft read it, provided a rationale for the mutual exploitation of the sexes when it dwelled on the influence women might wield by cultivating the art of pleasing. "I do not wish them to have power over men, but over themselves," was her tart reply. Rousseau's "philosophy of lasciviousness," which the *Vindication* was expressly designed to refute, would make women "beautiful, innocent, and silly." The education Rousseau prescribed for women amounted to a series of "preparations for adultery." It perpetuated the "state of war which subsists between the sexes." Wollstonecraft's program, on the other hand, would promote mutual respect, the only basis on which men and women could meet as equals.

She objected to the cult of love, in part, because love was necessarily evanescent. Since it was a passing thing, passion could never serve as the basis of stable attachments. That it was held in high esteem indicated only that neither women nor aristocrats could see beyond the "present moment." When passion cooled, those raised only for love gave way to "jealousy and vanity" or sought other lovers. Feminine arts were "only useful to a mistress." In a proper marriage the "fever" of love gave way to a "healthy temperature." "Coquettish arts" stood in the way of this transition, but where esteem prevailed, men and women were "contented to love but once in their lives, and after marriage let passion subside into friendship." Friendship alone, Wollstonecraft insisted again and again, could sustain men and women when "beauty fades" and the "giddy whirl of pleasure" began to pall. "When the lover becomes a friend," marriage comes into its own. A decent reserve on both sides, mutual "esteem, the only lasting affection," and economic independence for both partners added up to Wollstonecraft's recipe for a happy marriage.[2]

In stressing the common ground occupied by Hannah More and Mary Wollstonecraft, I do not mean to neglect the differences between them. Wollstonecraft's two novels, in both of which the heroine finds herself married to a man she cannot love and ends by committing adultery, were enough to put her beyond the pale of respectable opinion. There was a romantic, headstrong streak in Wollstonecraft that ran counter to the *Vindication*'s tribute to friendship. Failing to follow her own sensible advice, she repeatedly found herself embroiled in unrequited affairs until she finally settled down with the prosaic Godwin, whose domestic life turned out to be as stolid as his writings were romantic and inflammatory. Her tragic history gave her the reputation of a loose woman or—for a growing list of admirers—of a wise woman far ahead of her times.

On the contrary, Wollstonecraft's work was deeply embedded in her times—in the middle-class critique of "fashion," in the redefinition of marriage as a meeting of friends, in the insistence on friendship as the emotional basis of equality. Far from promoting sexual warfare in the manner of the *précieuses*, Wollstonecraft, no less than Hannah More, wished to bring it to a close. In some ways her work looked backward to an earlier epoch in the history of the middle class, in which women worked alongside their husbands on farms or small shops and had neither time nor inclination for romantic intrigue. There is no question that she was a radical egalitarian, but what matters, from our point of view, is that she found no inconsistency between egalitarianism and middle-class marriage. To be sure, she advocated liberalization of the divorce laws, but so had John Milton, another defender of the married state. There was no suggestion, in Wollstonecraft's writings, that marriage was by its very nature a prison for women. She regarded it instead as the highest form of friendship, hence an inherently egalitarian arrangement, a partnership that gave full scope to women's abilities. As long as women served only an ornamental purpose, they could not aspire to this marital ideal.

Throughout the nineteenth century this critique of "fashion" remained the moral touchstone of middle-class marriage. Feminists and antifeminists alike, bitterly divided about everything else, joined Wollstonecraft and More in condemning the doctrine that woman's highest aim was to please. In the United States, as in England, the scramble for wealth and status created a middle class seemingly determined to revive the worst practices of a discredited aristocracy. The revival of aristocratic manners appeared all the more threatening in a society officially committed to democracy. Critics of "fashion" identified themselves at once with the triumphant progress of republican ideals and, in a more alarmist mood, with the defense of old-fashioned virtues menaced with extinction by the growth of a commercial elite bent on matching the European aristocracies in profligate display and loose living. A century and a half of Calvinist preaching on the moral declension of the early religious settlements in New England made this retrospective style of social commentary attractive to Americans, almost habitual. Benjamin Rush, a man of the Enlightenment, easily fell into the manner of the Puritan jeremiad when he noted "how differently modern writers and the inspired author of the proverbs, describe a fine woman." The moral advantage, he went on to make clear, was all on the side of the proverbs, now observed principally in the breach.

> [Modern writers] confine their praises chiefly to personal charms, and ornamental accomplishments, while [the proverbs] celebrate only the virtues of a valuable mistress of a family, and a useful member of society. The one is perfectly acquainted with all the fashionable languages of Europe; the other, "opens her mouth with wisdom," and is perfectly acquainted with all the uses of the needle, the distaff, and the loom. The business of the one, is pleasure, the pleasure of the other, is business. The one is admired abroad; the other is honored and beloved at home.

Earlier in the same tract, *Thoughts on Female Education*, Rush linked the domestic virtues to the overthrow of monarchy and the achievement of American independence. Changes in the structure of society had produced corresponding changes in family life, as a result of which "the education of young ladies, in this country, should be conducted upon principles very different . . . from what it was when we were a part of a monarchical empire." Aristocratic society rested on leisure and display, middle-class society on work. "In Britain, company and pleasure are the principal business of ladies, and the nursery and the kitchen form no part of their daily cares." In America, on the other hand—thanks in part to the shortage of domestic servants—middle-class women not only took over the "principal share of the instruction of children" but were expected to help their husbands in their business. Their education, Rush thought, ought to prepare them for these arduous but by no means exclusively domestic duties. They should learn figures and bookkeeping, penmanship, English grammar (as opposed to foreign languages), history, and the essentials of home management. Rush did not completely rule out dancing or training in vocal music, but he recommended dancing merely as a useful form of exercise, music as preparation for psalm singing and for soothing with a song "the cares of domestic life."

Many historians have interpreted the cult of domesticity as a backward step in the march of progress, a reaction against the revolutionary demands that emerged during the political upheavals of the late eighteenth century. It is important to remind ourselves, therefore, that feminists and antifeminists agreed on a central point: that women should make themselves useful instead of cultivating the art of sexual attraction. By 1837 Sarah Josepha Hale, editor of *Godey's Lady's Book* (which could hardly be considered a feminist publication), could remark with satisfaction on the "great change . . . in public opinion respecting the estimation in which the influence of women should be held." The recognition of her "vast moral power," Mrs. Hale believed, would lead to programs of education "appropriate to her character and duties," as a result of which woman would "no longer deserve or incur from [men] the epithet of 'romantic animal.' " Fashionable education, on the other hand, had as its object an eligible match—the marketing of female sexuality at the highest possible price.

No pains or expense is spared to make a *lady* of mamma's daughter, as she may some time be mistress of a splendid establishment, conveying the idea that it is a "consumma-tion devoutly to be wished"; and she should be prepared to do the honors gracefully. Her education, so far as books are concerned, is superficial; but she has been thoroughly drilled in what "mamma" terms the accomplishments; that is, she can waltz like a dancing-master; the studied grace of her manner is perfection; in dress, her taste is faultless; and in flirting she may be rivalled, but not surpassed. And all this training has been to fit her for the *duties of life*; not as the phrase goes, that she may make "some good man a wife," but that she may secure a desirable husband.

The young girl exposed to a fashionable upbringing came to believe that "matrimony is the only thing in the world that woman can look to with the hope of securing an honorable position in society." In challenging this view—in urging that "a little more self-dependence" and knowledge of the world would enable a woman "to grace any station in which she might be placed"—Mrs. Hale in 1858 was aware that "sensi-ble" opinions would be dismissed in fashionable circles as antiquated. Aristocratic patterns of social life, it appeared, had reestablished themselves in America without much dif-ficulty, and the champions of common sense repeatedly com-plained, with a mixture of alarm and complacency, that their ideas were now regarded as hopelessly out-of-date. "I despise fashionable life," says the hero of a story of the 1830s, typical of the fiction preferred by *Godey's*, "and would rather wed a shrew than a fashionable girl. . . . Though you may laugh at my obsolete ideas of a wife, . . . when I choose, it must be one who will make her husband's home to him the sunny spot of earth." William A. Alcott, in his *Young Woman's Guide to Excellence*, explained that he preferred "the good old

fashioned term, YOUNG WOMAN" to "lady," since the latter suggested "exemption from labor, and of entire devotion
to something supposed to be above it—as fashionable company, or fashionable dress and equipage."

This kind of talk could be pushed to the feminist conclusions Mrs. Hale and other domestic moralists were so eager
to avoid. Once "maternal influence" came to be seen as the
most effective antidote to fashionable dissipation, it was hard
to explain why that influence should be confined to the
home. The world cried out for reform, and women's gift for
domesticity by no means disqualified them from this
important work. Just the reverse: It created an obligation to
put the domestic virtues at the service of society as a whole.
The family, in any case, could not be sheltered from outside
influences—alcoholism, prostitution, the speculative mania,
the mad scramble for wealth. Because these evils impinged
on the family, a conscientious housewife, it could be argued,
had to join in the public agitation against them, if only to
secure her own domain. As early as the 1820s and 1830s
women began to organize moral reform societies dedicated
to the abolition of the influences that tended to undermine
family life. The temperance movement, in particular, enlisted
the energies of thousands of women and established itself as a
more or less permanent force in nineteenth-century politics.
When critics objected that political participation would
"unsex" women, the women stood their ground. A group of
evangelical clergymen took it upon themselves to organize a
campaign against sexual promiscuity and advised the New
York Female Reform Society (founded in 1834) that it could
safely leave this work to men, only to be told, in no uncertain
terms, that "this is the appropriate work for women." The
Advocate, the society's journal, advanced feminist arguments
well before the official founding of the women's rights move-

ment in 1848: "We allude to the tyranny exercised in the HOME department, where lordly man, 'clothed in a little brief authority,' rules his trembling subjects with a rod of iron, conscious of his entire impunity, and exalting in his fancied superiority. Instead of regarding his wife as a help-mate for him, an equal sharer in his joys and sorrows, he looks upon her as a useful article of furniture."

Often misinterpreted in our own time as a reactionary ideology designed to keep women in the kitchen, the cult of domesticity generated feminist thinking among women who did not necessarily think of themselves as feminists. Indeed it can be argued that feminism became an important force only when it mastered the idiom of domesticity and learned to reason from its premises instead of starting from the abstract premise of women's rights. Agitation for the rights of women implied that men and women were indistinguishable for all practical purposes or at least for the only purpose that mattered: whether or not women should be admitted to full citizenship. Many Americans, however, clearly found this way of thinking uncongenial. It minimized sexual differences and made no concessions to the growing belief in women's moral superiority.

Feminists themselves could not decide whether or not to base their case on sexual differences. In the 1850s they repeatedly debated this issue at their annual meetings. In reply to the claim that marriage represented the union of opposites, Lucretia Mott declared that "it is the union of similar, not opposite affections, which is necessary for the marriage bond." In Mrs. Mott's view, "mind has no sex"; women were rational creatures and enjoyed all the rights associated with reason. At a convention in Syracuse, in 1853, she dissented from the position advanced by Clarina Howard Nichols, that women's "moral susceptibilities are greater than those of man." Mrs. Mott "did not believe that women's moral feelings were more elevated than man's; but that with the same opportunities for development . . . there would probably be about an equal manifestation of virtue." Ernestine Rose likewise rejected arguments based on the "renovating influences of woman." The case for feminism, she maintained, had to rest not on expediency but on natural rights, specifically on the doctrine that taxation without representation flouted the political foundations of the American Republic.

Margaret Fuller's *Women in the Nineteenth Century*, the most important feminist treatise to appear before the Civil War, gave little comfort to those who wished to rest their case on woman's role as "regenerator of the world." Fuller argued that "feminine" and "masculine" traits could be found in the same individual—another way of saying that women's identity could not be encompassed in strictly sexual terms. Her thesis was clearly stated in the title she chose for the original version of her book when it appeared as an article in the *Dial* in the 1840s. Her title was cumbersome but highly suggestive: "The Great Lawsuit: Man versus Men, Woman versus Women." The root of the sexual problem, as Fuller saw it, was the substitution of abstractions for concrete experience. To abstract from women's varied experience a being called woman imprisoned the female sex in a set of stereotypes that precluded discussion of what women really were and might become. The stereotypes clustering around the image of "man" were no less confining, and it was in everyone's interest to break them down in favor of a more androgynous conception of human personality.

In the long run, however, the temptation to speak of woman in the abstract proved impossible to resist, least of all for feminists. In 1868 Elizabeth Cady Stanton published in her magazine, the *Revolution*, a speech by Lydia Becker, an English feminist, in which Becker denied the existence of intellectual differences between the sexes. Stanton added the revealing comment:

> We started on Miss Becker's ground twenty years ago, because we thought, from that standpoint, we could draw the strongest arguments for woman's enfranchisement. And there we stood firmly entrenched, until we saw that stronger arguments could be drawn from a difference in sex, in mind as well as body. . . . It is a low idea of sex to suppose it merely physical. Those who have known the joys of a true love and friendship, feel that there is sex in soul as well as body. . . . If a difference in sex involves superiority, then we claim it for woman.

Men were stern and unforgiving, Stanton continued; women, nurturant and full of mercy. "Thus far, the world has been governed by the masculine element, hence war, violence, fear, stern justice without mercy, governments and religions, alike based on force and fraud." If the "feminine element" had "asserted itself from the beginning, those governments of force and religions of damnation would have been modified long ago, mercy would have tempered justice, and love banished superstition." Neither capital punishment and war nor the concept of hell could have "emanated from the mother soul."

The immediate provocation behind this remarkable outburst, with its candid acknowledgment that "stronger arguments" had to prevail over principle and that feminists would be well advised to take up whatever line of reasoning promised political success, was the betrayal of feminists by their radical Republican allies. During the Civil War the radicals had committed themselves to a constitutional amendment enfranchising both freedmen and women. After the war, however, they decided to postpone agitation for woman suffrage on the grounds that Reconstruction was the "Negro's hour." Feminists, outraged, countered these arguments from expediency on their own ground. "Suffrage is a natural right," Stanton admitted, and hence required no further justification. "But when republicans and abolitionists claim that it is a political right, that citizens are to be enfranchised by classes, that 'this is the negro's hour,' then leaving the ground of principle, because they will not leave us there, and coming down to their low ground of expediency, we say 'educated women first, ignorant men afterward.' "

Stanton's anger was plain to see, but it would be a mistake to attribute the new line of argument exclusively to her quarrel with the radical Republicans. The real question is why "stronger arguments" for woman suffrage could now be drawn "from a difference in sex." If this perception was accurate—and there seems to be no reason to doubt it—it testified to a large-scale shift in public opinion, best described as a search for new models of national character. The long struggle against slavery, as we have seen, brought into the sharpest possible focus the issues informing the critique of patriarchal authority. Slavery exemplified everything reformers condemned under the name of fashion. Even defenders of slavery, sensitive to charges of sexual immorality and of "promiscuous" contacts between masters and slaves, began to embrace the growing consensus that self-discipline could be learned only in a well-ordered family setting in which the mother—not the patriarchal head of the household with his unlimited sexual privileges—played the principal disciplinary role. In a style reminiscent of Hannah More, Virginia Randolph Cary argued that "female influence" alone could check the "moral contagion" spread by promiscuous contact with slaves, thereby correcting the "deleterious influence of their example on the domestic circle." Hoping to reform slavery from within, in the same way that More sought to rescue the English middle classes from their own follies, Mrs. Cary urged the "mothers of Virginia" to forbid "all familiarity" between children and slaves and to see to it that their children did not become "infant despots" by "enforcing lawless authority over their allotted victims." Otherwise the slave regime might suffer the same fate that overtook the *ancien régime* in France, where the "state of the female sex" encouraged a general neglect of domestic duties. Instead of serving as the "active agents of moral improvement," the aristocratic woman made herself into a "mere ornament, a useless and superfluous toy."

Margaret Douglas, another southern writer, observed in an essay titled "The Influence of Slavery on the White Population" that white women in slaveholding societies were "too essentially indolent to undertake the arduous duty of 'managing' any thing or any body" and that they therefore consigned the "precious years of infancy . . . to the most ignorant and malicious hands."

Abolitionists added to this indigenous critique of slavery the important warning that societies founded on contempt for manual labor fostered such an ornamental view of womanhood unavoidably, regardless of the wishes of particular individuals who might seek to rise above the prevailing social restrictions. Southern women learned from their earliest youth to avoid labor and healthy exercise, abolitionists maintained, and their ingrained devotion to frivolous amusements disqualified them for the duties of wives and mothers. The rigid differentiation of sex roles, moreover, rested in a system of sexual segregation designed to safeguard the morals of women but conducive, in practice, to the very opposite result. Sexual segregation, according to George Bourne, "forms in them an artificial character, and by exciting the spirit of insatiable curiosity, renders them the easy prey of the colored girl, their attendant and associate, who ensnares the white female youth into an unhallowed acquaintance with the surrounding iniquity or into an unlawful connection with her colored brother, as a fair set-off for having been scourged and violated by the old slave-driver and his sons."

It is no wonder that feminists came to place so much emphasis on coeducation; the segregation of the sexes, in their eyes, gave rise to an unwholesome preoccupation with sex—the very condition it was designed to prevent. The frivolity and uselessness of the southern lady, her exaggerated interest in gossip and sexual scandal, her public flirtations, her clandestine intrigues—these were the mark of "fashion" carried to its extreme, a subjection less cruel, no doubt, but hardly less debilitating in its effects on character, according to abolitionists, than slavery itself. If the condition of women provided the best index of the progress of civilization—an idea almost universally held in the nineteenth century, repeated on every possible occasion—then the ornamental position of white women in the South, together with the general "harem-like aspect" of the large plantation, as abolitionists called it, stamped the South as a backward society, civilized in externals alone.

Whether or not this indictment had any basis in fact, it clearly resonated with the general tonality of nineteenth-century culture. If it contained large elements of pure fantasy, that made it all the more persuasive as a quasi-mythological construct, one that was played off, as William Taylor has demonstrated, against the contrasting image of the Yankee—industrious, enterprising, and supremely indifferent to the seductions of fashion. The northern victory in the Civil War ruled out the possibility, once and for all, that Americans would embrace an ethic of leisure as a national ideal, but the Cavalier ideal had already been repudiated, at least in the minds of most northerners, long before the attack on Fort Sumter. What was surprising, in the aftermath of the war, was the emergence of a body of opinion critical of the Yankee ideal itself.

Radicals like Wendell Phillips argued that reconstruction of the South implied a reconstruction of northern society. For Phillips, this implied an attack on the labor problem. Free labor, in the name of which the North had waged a bitter civil war, remained an empty ideal if it meant only the freedom to work for subsistence wages. A new breed of reformers, many of whom likewise had their roots in the antislavery movement, shared the belief that northern society needed rehabilitation. They gave this idea, however, a more conservative interpretation.

Disgusted with the corruption that flourished under the presidency of Grant, appalled by the widening rift between capital and labor, and fearful that the labor movement would model itself on the Paris Commune of 1870, these reformers identified reform not, as Phillips did, with the "producers" but with the "more well-to-do and observing classes," as E. L. Godkin, editor of the *Nation*, referred to them. Andrew Dickson White, president of Cornell, spoke for the new class of reformers when he deplored the amateurism, the ignorance of the "principles essential to public welfare" that characterized American politics. "In deciding public questions, exploded errors in political and social science are revamped, fundamental principles of law disregarded, and the plainest teachings of history ignored." Charles William Eliot sounded the same note in his 1869 inaugural address at Harvard, which he sought to make the training ground of a new administrative elite. "As a people," he said, "we have but a halting faith in special training for high professional employment." With a direct assault on the Yankee ideal, he went on to delineate the national danger.

> The vulgar conceit that a Yankee can turn his hand to anything we insensibly carry into high places, where it is preposterous and criminal. We are accustomed to seeing men leap from farm or shop to court-room or pulpit, and we half believe that common men can safely use the seven-league boots of genius. What amount of knowledge and experience do we habitually demand of our lawmakers? What special training do we ordinarily think necessary for our diplomatists?

Though it sought at least in part to mitigate the worst abuses of capitalism, the new professional and administrative elite relied on an equally destructive veneration of specialized training and expertise. The effort to curtail the market by means of an increasingly elaborate system of social services—the foundation of the welfare state—was self-defeating. It eroded everyday trust and competence and opened the family itself to bureaucratic intrusion. Widespread adherence to the notion that women's differences from men equipped them to reign over any activity considered domestic coincided with the growing reverence for professional guidance in even the most intimate matters. As a result, many women aligned with experts outside the family to buttress their authority. Meanwhile, feminists increasingly turned to sex differences to support their own case for the expansion of female prerogatives.

Hence the opposition to feminism, not very well articulated—opposition to a movement no longer satisfied with the appeal to civic equality. Early feminists argued for equality in matters where it was relevant. For the purpose of citizenship, it was pointless to argue about sex differences. When the argument from difference displaced the earlier line of argument, every facet of personal life was politicized. To politicize everything, however, is no better than to make everything into an object of exchange. While bourgeois domesticity and early feminism both began as critiques of social and economic inequality, the nineteenth century witnessed their abdication to new forms of elite dominance.

In the eighteenth and nineteenth centuries early feminists and antifeminists had attacked the view that women, through fashionable education, should dedicate themselves to a life of leisure and ornamentation. Both Hannah More and Mary Wollstonecraft, for instance, warned that mimicry of aristocratic ways rendered middle-class women unfit for their real obligations, discouraged self-sufficiency, and led to unproductive behavior. In the long run, however, their emphasis on virtue, serious work, and responsibility lost out to a kind of neopaternalism according to which women (and men too) depended on the assistance of specially trained professionals for the conduct of everyday life. The welfare state, Alan Wolfe shows, has forsaken its original purpose of redistributing income and has increasingly engaged in the regulation of moral obligations. State involvement at such a level diminishes the integrity of the family and other social institutions. It also undermines the cultivation of the very qualities the critics of fashion saw as indispensable for women. The ability to take seriously and to fulfill individual responsibilities in the process of living a productive life was the foundation stone for the attack on patriarchy, whether launched by feminists or antifeminists. The inability to do so is a source and sign of continued inequality, and worse. As Wolfe asks, "When government is relied on to furnish rules of moral obligation, will it weaken the very social ties that make government possible in the first place?"

NOTES

1. These observations shed further light on the eighteenth-century obsession with seduction, analyzed above in connection with the suppression of clandestine marriage. A young girl rich in "accomplishments" represented a considerable investment in the marriage market. She was not to be sacrificed to unscrupulous poachers or impecunious adventurers who refused to observe the proper conventions of courtship. But as Addison and Steele noted, the effect of her training was to make her a coquette—as such, fair game for seducers. Her training had as its object to make her attractive to men, but it was not easy for her—empty-headed young thing that she was—to distinguish counterfeiters from men with honorable intentions. These ironies, together with the emotional devastation to which they were all too likely to lead, became staple themes of the middle-class novel, beginning with Samuel Richardson and continuing through Jane Austen and George Meredith to Henry James.

2. When she spoke of economic independence, Wollstonecraft did not necessarily refer to paid work outside the home, except in the case of single women. She referred to the part women played in the domestic economy, which often called forth managerial skills of a high order. What she opposed was a system in which women did no useful work at all, making no contribution to the family income and becoming dependent, therefore, on what husbands chose to dole out. The household budget, she argued, should be a matter of mutual concern, as befitting a genuine partnership.

PART TWO

From Patriarchy to Neopaternalism

5

The Sexual Division of Labor, the Decline of Civic Culture, and the Rise of the Suburbs

The history of women, as the media have taught us to understand it, falls into two epochs, divided by the sexual revolution of the sixties. It was only in the sixties, according to the media's foreshortened view of things, that women began their painful climb out of the sexual dark ages. They entered the work force, gained control over their own bodies, and challenged male supremacy in all its forms—political, economic, ideological. Until then, women labored under age-old disabilities. Since the sixties, they have "come a long way," and although the revolution against patriarchy still has a long way to go before women gain full equality, it is irresistible. There can be no going back to the old days, to the "traditional" arrangements that kept women at home and left men in control of the great world outside.

It is this undifferentiated image of the old days that I want to call into question—the impression that women's lives used to be taken up entirely by the demands of housework and motherhood. In reality, full-time motherhood—the rejection of which touched off the latest wave of feminist agitation in the sixties—was something new and historically unprecedented. It was largely a product of the rapid growth of suburbs after World War II, and the feminist revival initiated by Betty Friedan's *The Feminine Mystique* originated as a direct response, often a very self-conscious response, not to the age-old oppression of women, but to the suburbanization of the American soul. Only later did the feminist movement come to understand the condition it sought to change—the division of labor that confined women to the home—as a "patriarchal" system that could be found, with minor variations, in all times and places. In the popular mind, the division of labor that prevailed in postwar suburbia thus came to be identified—with a corresponding loss of intellectual clarity—with the division of sexual labor in general.

All societies distinguish between women's work and men's work. Such distinctions are often invidious, serving to keep women in a subordinate status. It is only recently, however, that "woman's place" has been defined in such a way as to exclude her from participation in the common life beyond the household. The modern home, which presupposes a radical separation of domestic life from the world of work, was an invention of the nineteenth century. The decline of household production and the rise of wage labor made it possible— made it necessary—to conceive of the family as a private retreat from a public world increasingly dominated by the impersonal mechanisms of the market. The image of the family as a haven in a heartless world helped Americans to manage the ambivalent emotions evoked by the new industrial order. On the one hand, they wanted the comforts and conveniences furnished by industrial progress; on the other hand, the agency of progress—the capitalist market—appeared to foster a type of acquisitive individualism that left no room for the finer things in life: loving-kindness, spontaneous affection, what John Stuart Mill called the "culture of feelings." By assigning custody of "feelings" to the family, people tried to reassure themselves that values rooted in "ascription," as the sociologists say—recognition of persons that does not have to be earned but is merely bestowed—would continue to have a place even in societies governed by the principle of competitive achievement.

The nineteenth-century cult of domesticity, as historians have come to call it, revolved around a new glorification of motherhood. But the rhetoric of motherhood and domesticity cannot be taken as an accurate or complete description of women's lives in the nineteenth and early twentieth centuries. Housework and child care by no means exhausted women's energies. On the contrary, both housewives and single women threw themselves into a variety of activities that took them out of the home. They organized benevolent societies, female reform societies, and foreign missions. They put together a vast network of temperance societies. They took up charities and philanthropies of all kinds. Many of them enlisted in the antislavery crusade, the peace movement, prison reform, and of course the movement for women's rights. Historians have known for a long time that women played a central part in all the reform movements that swept over the country in the nineteenth century, not to mention the evangelical revivals that furnished much of the moral inspiration behind those movements; but they have somehow failed to connect these activities with the subject of women's work. For historians as for everybody else, work is understood as something dignified by a salary or a wage. Uncompensated activity, though it enters the historical record under the heading of "reform," is seldom recognized as a form of productive work, even when it brought women into the public world in great numbers. The impression that nineteenth-century women were confined to the domestic "sphere" thus remains undisturbed by the record of their active participation in the "world's work," as they themselves liked to refer to it.

Women's voluntary participation in the public world probably reached its high point in the years between 1890 and 1920, the so-called progressive era, which also coincided with the final stages of the campaign for woman suffrage. "Between 1890 and 1920," wrote the historian Mary Ryan, "women built a rationalized organizational network that was nearly as sophisticated in its own way as the corporate business world." The General Federation of Women's Clubs, organized in 1890, is estimated to have included two million members by 1910. Another two million took part in the movement for woman suffrage. In 1920, half a million women belonged to the Young Women's Christian Association, and almost a million to the Woman's Christian Temperance Union. The rapid growth of the National Council of Jewish Women, founded in 1893, indicates that the volunteering impulse was not confined to white Anglo-Saxon Protestants. The establishment of the National Association of Colored Women, in 1895, preceded the founding of the National Association for the Advancement of Colored People by fifteen years. The National Consumers League, the Women's Trade Union League, the Women's International League for Peace and Freedom, and innumerable other organizations, many of them now forgotten, enlisted the efforts of volunteers in a wide range of good causes. The progressive era was the age of "social housekeeping," when women aspired "to make the whole world homelike," in the words of Frances Willard of the WCTU. Women demanded the vote on the grounds that maternal "influence" should not be confined to the home. But they did not wait for the vote to legitimize their reforming efforts; nor were they handicapped by the lack of it. Indeed there is reason to think that women were more active citizens before getting the vote than afterwards, in part because they had so much stake in proving that they could act responsibly in the public realm. They took part in, and often initiated, movements to abolish child labor, to establish juvenile courts, to build slum housing, to require factory inspection, to strengthen the food and drug laws, and to abolish or regulate prostitution. "Scarcely without exception," according to Judge Ben Lindsey, one of the prominent reformers of the time, "it has been the members of the women's clubs . . . who have secured the passage of all the advanced legislation . . . for the protection of the home and the child."

Social reform was the most visible but by no means the exclusive or even the most important contribution made by women to public life. Their work as volunteers sustained a vast array of public services—libraries, hospitals, nursery schools, social settlements, parks, playgrounds, concert halls, museums. The progressive era was the heyday of the "city beautiful," when American cities built public facilities and amenities designed to bring culture to the masses and to encourage widespread participation in civic life. The reformer Frederic C. Howe spoke for his entire generation when he referred to the city as the "hope of democracy." Today it is fashionable to deprecate the civic architecture of those years as a monument to imperial grandeur and to sneer at "uplift" as an imposition of middle-class values on the immigrant poor. But uplift was not yet identified with "Americanization," and the public buildings that served to advertise America's commercial and military power also served to give ordinary people access to the nation's culture. Mary Antin, in her 1912 memoir of a girlhood spent in Russia and in the Jewish ghetto of South Boston, captured something of the promise of this urban awakening when she described the Boston Public Library as the "chamber of [her] dreams." With the carved inscription over its doors, "Built by the People— Free to All," the library brought home to her the "wonder of my life." "That I who was born in the prison of the Pale . . . [and] brought up to my teens almost without a book should be set down in the midst of all the books that ever were written was a miracle as great as any on record." No doubt Antin's account of immigrant life omitted some of its darker aspects, but it showed how much a great American city could offer to those who were able and willing to seize it.

These impressive resources, the foundations of which were laid down for the most part in the great age of American urbanism, were largely sustained, I suspect, by the unpaid labor of women, who raised the money, performed the daily drudgery, and furnished much of the moral vision behind the civic renewal of the early twentieth century. I am in no position to prove the point at this stage in my research, but it does not seem fanciful to suggest that it was women, toiling almost invariably behind the scenes and without monetary reward, who made the city liveable, prevented it from becoming a place devoted to business alone, and kept alive the vision of a civic culture open to all. Henry James observed, in *The American Scene* (1907), that the "interests of civilization," of "social property" and "social office," were carried on by women, while American men devoted themselves single-mindedly to business—that is, to private affairs, as they would have been described in Europe. Women, James wrote, had established "peerless possession" of all forms of public life in the true sense, of art, learning, and sociability; and although this arrangement—"the sentence written largest in the American sky"—struck him as deeply regrettable, since it meant that the "whole plane of the amenities" remained "residual" in a business civilization, it nevertheless provided Americans with as much civic culture as they had managed to achieve.

The American Scene, incidentally, contains a description of the Boston Public Library that should be set beside Mary Antin's. Comparing the new building in Copley Square to European libraries, James was struck by its accessibility, its rejection of any suggestion of the mystery or sacred space—*"penetralia"*—normally associated with a place of learning. A "library without *penetralia*" struck James as slightly incongruous, a "temple without altars." "The British Museum, the Louvre, the Bibliothèque Nationale, the Treasures of South Kensington, are assuredly . . . at the disposal of the people; but it is to be observed, I think, that the people walk there more or less under the shadow of the right waited for and conceded." The more democratic conception of culture embodied in the Boston Public Library, experienced by James as a "reservation" to his pleasure in the new building, was exactly what commended the place to a young woman from the slums.

James's misgivings about the democratization of culture may strike us as misplaced, but his account of the division of sexual labor provides a useful corrective to conventional accounts, which assume that unless women work in professional careers they must be confined to the home and which therefore miss women's contribution to an intermediate realm of civic culture that belongs neither to the family nor to the market. *The American Scene* is also useful, for our present purposes, because it enables us to see that the revulsion against the so-called genteel tradition, so clearly foreshadowed in James's book, was among other things a revulsion against the influence of women as custodians of American culture. In 1926, twenty years after the publication of *The American Scene*, Thomas Beer opened his influential little book *The Mauve Decade* with a savage attack on the "Titaness"—the American woman as arbiter of public taste and morals. By the 1890s, Beer wrote, "the Middle Western woman had quietly become a fixture on the American social chart, a shadowy Titaness, a terror to editors, the hope of missionary societies and the prey of lecturers." Animated by an "instinctive envy of all that was free, cool, or unhaltered," she had lost sight of whatever was "honourable in the Bostonian tradition," retaining only its "confusion of morals with manners." Together with "her more restrained sisters of the East and West," she tyrannized over the arts and made politicians tremble with her many-sided campaign for "social purity." No lapse of taste or decorum was too small to escape her attention, according to Beer. "She was an emblem, a grotesque shape in hot black silk, screaming threats at naked children in a clear river, with her companionable ministers and reformers at heel." She attended "congress after congress for the correction of mankind." Her censorship of literature bespoke a "resolute violence of the cheapest kind, without breeding, without taste." No doubt she did not invent "cheap cruelty and low social pressures," but she "erected these basenesses into virtues by some defensive sense of rectitude, and a generation of sons was reared in the shadow of the Titaness, aware of her power, protected by nothing from her shrill admonitions."

It took more than satire, whether in the form of Beer's venom or the gentler ridicule of Helen Hokinson, to drive women out of the public forum, but satire must have played some part in their postwar retreat from civic causes and campaigns. In the twenties, club women, do-gooders, "upbuilders," and cultural missionaries became symbols of Victorian repression or, at best, figures of fun. The flapper, not the feminist, now served as the prototype of the emancipated woman; the battle of the sexes shifted from the lecture circuit to the bedroom; and the assertion of women's equal right to sexual pleasure absorbed energies formerly devoted to social reform and civic improvement. The professionalization of these activities further contributed to the decline of voluntary public service. Settlement houses were taken over by professional social workers, charities by professional administrators. A sociological investigation carried out many years later, *Life Styles of Educated Women*, by Eli Ginzberg and his associates, reported that "volunteer organizations have come more and more under the control and direction of full-time professional staff. While there is still a place for the volunteer either as a board member or as a worker, the scope for her participation in many organizations has been substantially reduced." The same consideration led Morton Hunt, in his 1962 study of American women, *Her Infinite Variety*, to conclude that although "perhaps ten to fifteen million women do volunteer work for various community agencies," these impressive numbers "mean less than they seem to." Voluntary service had never recovered the prestige it enjoyed in the nineteenth and early twentieth centuries. Women now had to choose between a home and a career, and the choice had become so familiar that people soon forgot that there had ever been any other.

Volunteer work commended itself to women, in the age of its efflorescence, in part because it was easily combined with domestic responsibilities, unlike the inflexible schedules imposed by paid work. Those responsibilities, moreover, were themselves less burdensome than they subsequently became, since most women were able to count on help from domestic servants, in-laws and relatives, and their own children. The "benevolent empire" of nineteenth-century women, including the feminist movement itself, "was underwritten by the household labors of domestic servants," as Faye Dudden noted in her study of household service, *Serving Women*. In the twentieth century, however, live-in domestic servants gradually disappeared from American households, except from those of the very rich, and even part-time servants grew harder and harder to find. Immigration restriction, compulsory education, and the availability of less demeaning jobs in factories and offices choked off the supply of domestics, while new standards of domestic privacy (together with a drastic shrinkage in the size of middle-class houses) made the employment of live-in servants seem undesirable in any case. But the decline of domestic service was not the only development that altered the structure of the American household. In the past, the household economy always rested, in part, on the exchange of unpaid services among relatives, friends, and neighbors, as Mary Howell reminded us some years ago in her unjustly neglected little book *Helping Ourselves: Families and the Human Network*. Household tasks, including child care, were typically shared by a network of women who were in a position to make claims on each other's good will. It was precisely because this system relied on mutual trust that it worked as well as it did, according to

Howell; but it was this same element of trust and mutual obligation, in all likelihood, that eventually discredited the barter system of domestic management in the minds of people who came to experience any form of personal obligation primarily as a limitation on their own freedom. To depend on others puts us under obligation to them, whereas the impersonal mechanism of the market enables us to satisfy all our obligations by the simple act of payment. The desire to escape obligation, even more than an exaggerated respect for professional expertise, explains the professionalization of domestic services formerly carried out informally and without payment. "We have grown far from a formally approved system of barter for unpaid services," Howell observed. "We wonder if it is not more civilized, more sophisticated . . . to pay for what we need. A barter system . . . must rely on human frailty and human good will."

The barter system presupposed the existence of stable urban neighborhoods, in which long-time residents knew enough about their neighbors to trust them, to call on them for help, and to build up reciprocal obligations of their own. The proximity of relatives and in-laws, another prerequisite of any system of unpaid exchange, was another feature of such neighborhoods. As urban sociologists have often pointed out, close-knit neighborhoods, often based on a strong sense of ethnic identity, preserved some of the features of village life in the midst of large cities. Even when the household ceased to be a unit of production, it was still bound to the surrounding community by ties of mutual obligation. The "isolation of the nuclear family"—another theme of urban sociology—was qualified by neighbors' dependence on each other for all kinds of domestic services. "Isolation" was a better description of the suburban than of the urban family; and it was the rapid expansion of suburbs, beginning in the 1940s and 1950s, that finally destroyed the social patterns I have tried to sketch in here—the informal system of collective self-help that made it possible, together with the availability of domestic servants, for women to take an active part in civic culture—and inaugurated a new era in the history of women and the family. Suburban life, organized around the shopping mall rather than the neighborhood, eradicated the last vestiges of reciprocal obligation, neighborly or familial; and it is important to see that this was precisely what made it attractive. It was not just the lure of green lawns and open spaces that drew people to the suburbs but the dream of perfect freedom, of a world in which the demands of your relatives and neighbors would be vastly reduced (if not eliminated altogether) and your time would be entirely your own.

It is often said that people went to the suburbs in search of "community," as an alternative to urban anonymity. I think it was just the other way around. What they craved was complete privacy—the freedom to bring up their children without interference from intrusive relatives and neighbors, to choose their friends on the basis of mutual interests instead of physical proximity, and to organize their time without consulting the pleasure or convenience of anyone else. Suburbs appeared to institutionalize the principle of free and unlimited choice. They were designed to exclude everything not subject to choice—the job, the extended family, the enforced sociability of the city streets. Americans hoped to put all that behind them when they headed for the seclusion of the suburbs, where they were accountable, it seemed, to no one.

It was in the suburbs, much more than in the city, that women became full-time mothers and homemakers. The traditional family, so called, where the husband goes out to work and the wife stays home with the children, was not traditional at all. It was a mid-twentieth-century innovation, the product of a growing impatience with external obligations and constraints, of the equation of freedom with choice, and of tumultuous world events that made the dream of a private refuge in the suburbs more and more appealing. The idea that domestic life would provide such a refuge had a longer history, of course, but it was only in the postwar suburbs that it came close to realization. The family could plausibly be described as a "holy refuge," an "oasis far from the maddening throng," a "bastion against depersonalization and dehumanization," a "fortress," an "island of serenity and support and understanding in a hectic, plastic, often avaricious world," only in suburbs founded on the separation of the home not merely from the workplace but from outside influences of any kind. Domestic servants, extended family members, friends and neighbors acting as an informal support system—all were excluded from the middle-class suburban household, with the result that housewives found themselves in sole possession, free at last to arrange things exactly as they pleased.

It did not take long for this freedom to pall. By the early sixties (if not before), the "holy refuge" of the suburban family came to be experienced as a "comfortable concentration camp," in Betty Friedan's memorable phrase. *The Feminine Mystique*, published in 1963, launched a new wave of feminist agitation, which has changed the American landscape far more deeply than earlier waves—to the point where everything that took place before the sixties is now consigned to the era of the "traditional family." What is striking about Friedan's manifesto, when one returns to it more than thirty years later, is the degree to which it was dominated by the plight of suburban women. Friedan pointed out that the

"explosive movement to the suburbs"—"those ugly and endless sprawls which are becoming a national problem"—coincided with a "great increase in the numbers of educated
women choosing to be just housewives." It did not seem
unreasonable to interpret the "postwar suburban explosion"
as the product of a "mistaken choice" made by a new generation of women who repudiated the active life of their predecessors and saw the family as a refuge from increasingly
unmanageable conditions in the public world. Women with
"commitments outside the home," Friedan observed, were
"less likely to move to the suburbs"; but such women
appeared to be a dying breed. Women brought up in an earlier day, even as late as the thirties and early forties, did not
regard themselves exclusively as housewives. Eighty percent
of the women who graduated from Smith in the early forties,
as Friedan discovered when she took a survey of her own
class of 1943, "had found some way to pursue the goals that
education had given them," usually in the form of "community activity" as volunteers. After the war, however, the suburbs began to attract a "new breed of women" who were
"looking for sanctuary" and were "perfectly willing to fill their
days with the trivia of housewifery." "Women of this kind,"
according to Friedan, refused "to take policy-making positions in community organizations," leaving the "really interesting volunteer jobs" to be filled by men. They justified their
"resistance to serious community responsibility" on the
grounds that their families took all their time. Since housework and child care did not absorb their "full capacities,"
however, they soon developed the symptoms familiar to students of the "problem that has no name"—chronic fatigue,
boredom, loneliness, and a "nameless aching dissatisfaction"
they sought to relieve with alcohol, drugs, overeating, sexual
adventures, or an obsessive interest in their children.

Except that it focused on women, Friedan's book closely resembled many other accounts of suburban life, almost all of which deplored "conformity, status-seeking, [and] escape," in Friedan's words. Like many other commentators, Friedan worried about the effects of excessive maternal attention on children growing up in suburbia, especially on boys. "A subtle and devastating change," she wrote, "seems to have taken place in the character of American children." Their lives seemed empty and pointless. "Apathetic, dependent, infantile, purposeless," these children had no consuming interests or goals. There was "nothing these kids felt strongly enough about to die for." They had no ambition, no taste for competition, and no capacity for hard work or physical endurance. Accustomed to having all their wants provided for by others, they lacked "self-sufficiency." They suffered from "passivity," "softness," "muscular deterioration." Many of the young men became homosexuals, driven by an "implacable hatred for the parasitic women who keep their husbands and sons from growing up." There was a definite link, Friedan thought, "between what is happening to the women in America and increasingly overt male homosexuality." Homosexuality, which was "spreading like a murky smog over the American scene," was "no less ominous than the restless, immature self-seeking of the young women who are the aggressors in . . . early marriages." The ease with which American prisoners in Korea were brainwashed by their captors provided further evidence of a "parasitical softening" in the American character. So did the rise of the "bearded, undisciplined beat generation"—a "singularly passionless and purposeless form of adolescent rebellion." Many other observers of American life, Friedan noted, had come to the same conclusion: that "these new kids are . . . not growing up 'real.' "

One of the most discerning of these observers, Paul

Goodman, brought out his *Growing Up Absurd* in 1960, just three years before the publication of *The Feminine Mystique*. Although nobody seems to have noticed this at the time, the two books complemented each other quite closely: Each emphasized an important dimension of the problem that was ignored by the other. They agreed in their description of the problem—the difficulty of growing up in a world that made few demands on one's intelligence or strength of character. Like Friedan, Goodman regarded the emergence of the beat generation as an important symptom of the passivity and resignation that were spreading through American society. His portrait of the beats was more sympathetic than Friedan's but no less depressing. Those who called themselves beat, as Goodman saw them, had plenty of reasons for refusing to grow up into the roles they were expected to fill as adults. But their "defensive ignorance of the academic culture," together with their "cynicism and neglect of ethical and political goals," condemned their rebellion to futility. They experienced the university "as a part of the worthless organized system rather than as Newton and Virgil." Accordingly, their literary culture remained parochial and undeveloped, dependent on the illusion that it was self-sufficient and could dispense with exposure to the larger world of letters. The beats wrote for an audience too easily impressed by third-rate work, a "somewhat sickening audience because it has no objective cultural standard." Having cut themselves off from the "stream of ancient and international tradition," they tried "to make the parochial the *only* existing culture" and thus to make themselves artists by definition. But mutual admiration was a poor substitute for the kind of artistic, literary, and intellectual achievement that could be validated by objective standards. "The artist finds that he is a parochial group hero, when the reassurance that he needs, if he is diffident, is that he is a culture hero for the immortal world." The beats' characteristic expressions of mutual praise and encouragement—"It's the greatest!" "Go, man, go!"—carried little conviction. "In a milieu of resignation, where the young men think of society as a closed room in which there are no values but the rejected rat race or what they can produce out of their own guts, it is extremely hard to aim at objective truth or world culture."

According to Goodman, the beats rejected the prevailing definition of success—money, possessions, a house in the suburbs—but shared the general conviction "that society cannot be different." Having no large hopes, they could not escape the general condition of young men "growing up absurd"—apathy, disappointment, and cynicism. The root of the difficulty was that the "organized system," as Goodman called it, did "not want men"; instead it wanted hucksters, promoters, timeservers, and entertainers. It subordinated the production of useful goods and services to the sale of commodities designed to wear out quickly, to be superseded by changes in fashion, to appeal to the public's jaded appetite for novelty, or to satisfy a desire for the social status conferred by conspicuous display. Young men wanted to feel useful, but the available jobs required them to produce and market useless consumer goods, as opposed, say, to "necessary food and shelter." A young man might choose to become an auto mechanic—a seemingly useful line of work—only to find that "cars have a built-in obsolescence" and that "manufacturers do not want them to be repaired or repairable." Under these conditions, "his feelings of justification, sociability, serviceability" were likely to dissolve. It was "not surprising" if he became "cynical and time-serving, interested in a fast buck."

This kind of experience was bound to be repeated over and over again, according to Goodman, in a society that maintained its "so-called high standard of living" by turning out commodities that no one really needed. Opponents of the New Deal had pointed out the demoralizing effects of "make-work," but the whole economy now depended on work that had no other object than to keep people at work and thus to sustain the national "capacity to consume," which in turn sustained production, which sustained full employment (or an approximation of full employment)—all without reference to the intrinsic quality of the goods and services produced or the intrinsic satisfaction of the work that went into them. The vicious circle of a consumer economy made the popular perception of the workaday world as a rat race quite appropriate. Such an economy deprived young men of the kind of work they could "enthusiastically and spontaneously throw themselves into" and thus denied them any compelling incentive to grow up at all. The ideal of "having a real job that you risk your soul in" belonged to the "heroic age of capitalist enterprise." In the new world of make-work and planned obsolescence, young men could no longer believe either in the jobs they were expected to grow up into or in the country as a whole. In the past, "there was always something special in the American destiny to be proud of." The increasingly narrow identification of the American dream with the American standard of living, however, extinguished the spirit of patriotism just as effectively as the consumer economy extinguished the spirit of workmanship.

Throughout his book, Goodman repeatedly referred to the importance of "man's work" in conferring "manly independence" and a manly character. He had next to nothing to say about young women; in a book that otherwise seems as timely today as it did thirty years ago, this silence is the only feature that is likely to strike us as curiously outdated. Goodman simply assumed, without giving the matter much thought, that housekeeping and child care were useful jobs in the nature of things—the kinds of jobs that promoted self-esteem and a sense of accomplishment. This was so widely understood, according to Goodman, that men themselves had begun to embrace domesticity as a "secondary but real career." The "new fatherhood" that was taking shape in the fifties, he argued, was another indication of their disenchantment with the rat race. Whereas Friedan deplored the revival of domesticity and the flight to the suburbs, Goodman saw these developments, quite erroneously I think, as an "important new effort toward community." The new suburban "settlements" devoted "time and energy to common interests." The "improvement of the child's world" led to "genuine community participation, committee meetings and lectures on psychology, concern for traffic and zoning, and even extension courses in cultural subjects to create the proper atmosphere for growing up."

At this point, Goodman's analysis badly needed a feminist corrective. Child rearing may be an honorable calling, but many women clearly found it increasingly unsatisfactory in the fifties and sixties, and it was important to understand the reasons for this—the reasons that were to make them so receptive to Friedan's attack on the "feminine mystique." Her own explanation was quite consistent with Goodman's account of the corruption of work, although she made no reference to it. She pointed out that housekeeping and child care had themselves taken on many of the telltale characteristics of make-work. Once women gave up extrafamilial interests, "housewifery expanded to fill the time available." Women lavished more attention on domestic duties than those duties really required (or than was good for children). Like much of the work men performed in the marketplace, these duties appeared to have no other purpose than to keep women busy. Child care, moreover, was important only if it was connected with larger public purposes. Goodman himself conceded the substance of this point when he noted—though only in passing—that when adults devoted themselves exclusively to the child's world, "there isn't much world for the child to grow up into in the next stage." In order for a father "to guide his growing son," it was "necessary for him to have a community of his own and be more of a man." But the same thing was surely true of women. That this obvious point should have escaped attention until Betty Friedan made it inescapable shows why the feminist revival was necessary in the first place. Without it, even the most astute analysis of the difficulties of growing up in America would remain partial and one-sided.

But Friedan's analysis was one-sided in its own right without the kind of corrective provided by Goodman. His account of the world of work should have forewarned women that they would not gain much simply by entering the work force and achieving equality with men. Once women had rejected the "feminine mystique," it was tempting to think that professional careers would solve all their problems. From the point of view of the "comfortable concentration camp," the masculine world of competitive achievement looked glamorous and exciting (just as suburban domesticity looked warm and reassuring to men disaffected with the rat race). Women accordingly began to demand access to the allegedly "creative," "fulfilling" work enjoyed by men. They did not argue simply that it was both risky and demeaning to depend entirely on a man for support. They expected professional careers to bring them emotional fulfillment. If Goodman was right, however, they would find no more meaning than men did in careers the structure of which was governed largely by the requirements of commodity production. Goodman's point was not the conventional one that most jobs involved too much drudgery and routine and thus provided an inadequate outlet for "creativity." His point was that they did not produce anything of importance and were therefore dishonorable and demoralizing. From this point of view, a career as a highly paid lawyer, advertising executive, broadcast journalist, or college professor was even more demoralizing, if it served only to maintain the "organized system," than a job as an auto mechanic, which did not even pretend to be useful. This was an argument women very much needed to hear; otherwise they too would fall into the careerist trap. They needed to be reminded that good work was useful work, not glamorous or "stimulating" or "creative" work, and that its usefulness, moreover, could not be measured by a wage or salary.

Nothing in *The Feminine Mystique* was inconsistent with such a view of work, any more than *Growing Up Absurd* was incompatible with a feminist perspective on the domestic revival. One of the surprises in store for anyone who returns to Friedan's best-seller today is how little she was inclined to identify the work women ought to be doing with highly paid professional careers. She wanted women to get out of the house, but she did not necessarily want them to throw themselves into the job market. No doubt she was too quick to characterize the kind of work she had in mind as "creative," and her insistence that it should put a college education to good use reveals her lack of interest in working-class women; but at least she did not confuse "creativity" with payment. She urged women to find "work, paid or unpaid, requiring initiative, leadership and responsibility." What mattered was a "lifelong commitment," not a career as such—a commitment to "society" at that. Women had to "make their contribution not as 'housewives' but as citizens." All too often, however, they stepped "back from . . . volunteer activity . . . at the very point when all that is needed is a more serious commitment." "The PTA leader won't run for the school board. The League of Women Voters' leader is afraid to move on into the rough mainstream of her political party." If Friedan preferred paid to unpaid work, on the whole, it was only because "being paid . . . implies a definite commitment" and because a "no-nonsense nine-to-five job . . . requires less discipline" than a more flexible schedule. Volunteer work, on the other hand, required self-discipline, dedication, and a talent for improvisation—qualities that were almost always in short supply.

Because the women's movement—the movement Friedan's book helped to launch—has repudiated volunteer work as the very epitome of female slavery, it is easy to miss her emphasis on citizenship and "commitment." In the sixties and seventies, this way of talking about women gave way to an ostensibly more radical, hardheaded idiom. Women could never be free, feminists argued, until they were able to compete with men in the job market, and successful competition appeared to require institutional reforms—affirmative action, unlimited abortion rights, a comprehensive program of day care financed by public funds—that went far beyond the modest reforms advocated by *The Feminine Mystique*. Friedan herself later took the position that "without child care, women will never really advance in their careers." In the light of the subsequent radicalization of the women's movement, *The Feminine Mystique* is usually read (when it is read at all) as the first halting step down the road since traveled by an army of more militant women. But it may make more sense to read it, alongside Goodman's book, as an attempt to mark out a road that was later abandoned. These books addressed the same issue, at bottom, even though they approached it in different ways. The issue, in a word, was how to revive a sense of vocation in a society destitute of any sense of common purpose. Like Goodman, Friedan believed that "women, as well as men, can only find their identity in work that uses their full capacities." But neither women nor men, it seems, could find such work in the brave new world of postwar suburbia. Hailed as the fulfillment of the American dream, the suburbs had turned into an American nightmare. Perhaps the most revealing commentary on the new order of the suburbs, an order based on a strict separation between the home and the workplace and a strict division of sexual labor, was that each sex envied the lives led by the other. Men envied the domestic security supposedly enjoyed by their wives; women envied the exciting careers supposedly enjoyed by their husbands. As for their children—supposedly the ultimate beneficiaries of suburban life, whose needs the whole system was intended to serve—their aimless, pampered existence had come to be regarded as a national scandal. Goodman was not alone in his insistence that young men were growing up "without high aims and with little sense of a natural or moral community." He was not alone in observing "how rarely one hears, even delivered unctuously, the mention of some lofty purpose." Many other critics of American society made the same observation in the late fifties and early sixties, though none explained so clearly why this absence of collective purpose made it so hard for young men to grow up. The effect of Friedan's book, considered in this context, ought to have been to discourage any lingering hope that young women were growing up any better than young men and at the same time to make it clear that the difficulties faced by women were not faced by women alone. "Why aren't girls forced to grow up?" Friedan asked. Because they had "no goal, no purpose, no ambition." But if the same thing could be said of young men, careers for women could hardly provide any more than a small part of the solution.

My purpose in saying this is not to urge women to abandon the workplace or to force them into a position of economic dependence but merely to point out that professional careers are no more liberating for women than for men if those careers are governed by the requirements of the corporate economy. As long as the workplace is dominated by the need to sustain economic growth by producing goods and services no one really needs, it will be unable to satisfy the desire to become not just self-supporting but useful and self-respecting. Nor will the employment of women transform the workplace, as feminists often promise. Putting women in charge of corporations, law firms, newspapers, publishing houses, TV stations, universities, and hospitals does not make those institutions more democratic and humane. It does not soften the masculine drive for competitive achievement with the feminine gift for friendly cooperation. It does not make capitalist institutions more loving and maternal. Those institutions have a life of their own, quite independent of the qualities of the people who manage them. They obey the laws of the market, not the golden rule. They have only one overriding aim, to show a profitable return on investment; everything else is incidental. Under corporate capitalism, use value will always remain secondary to exchange value. Under the economic conditions that prevail today, the connection between them is even more tenuous than it was in the past. Financial speculation has become far more profitable than production, and production itself is driven by marketing strategies that rely on the familiar technique of planned obsolescence. Advertising, the quintessential art form in late capitalist societies, seeks to encourage a taste for novelty and to create dissatisfaction with anything old or out-of-date. Its ideal is a world of disposable goods, where things are discarded as soon as they have lost their initial appeal. That anything should be repaired, restored, or renewed is foreign to the advertising ethic, which invokes the myth of technological progress in order to reinforce the idea that commodities advertised as new and revolutionary, upgraded and improved, are necessarily superior to the ones they drive out of the market. Often the "improvement" is purely cosmetic, but even when it serves some purpose, it usually defeats one that is equally important. The word processor is not an unambiguous improvement over the typewriter, but it puts the typewriter out of business, just as private motor cars have replaced other forms of transportation that were better suited to certain purposes. The replacement of long-playing records by compact discs, of silent films by talkies, of ocean liners by airplanes, of midwives by obstetricians, of neighborhood stores by shopping malls, of voting by public opinion polls illustrates the same point—that new technologies and the practices that grow up around them tend to become monopolies in an economy that relies so heavily on the principle of enforced obsolescence to sustain high levels of growth. Instead of expanding the range of social and private choice, as enthusiasts of innovation constantly assert, new technologies force consumers to accept what the market dictates. The celebration of choice, another important element in the ideology of progress and consumption, obscures the restriction of choice to the latest innovations, whether or not they answer the purposes they allegedly aim to satisfy.

Women's entry into the work force does not change any of this. The feminist movement, far from civilizing corporate capitalism, has been corrupted by it. It has adopted mercantile habits of thought as its own. Its relentless propaganda against the "traditional" family is of a piece with the propaganda of commodities, which encourages the consumer to discard arrangements that are still serviceable only because they are said to lag behind the times. Like the advertising industry, the women's movement has taken "choice" as its slogan, not only in the matter of abortion but in its attack on the old-fashioned family, now held to be only one of a variety of family types among which people may freely choose. In fact, however, the movement recognizes only one choice— the family in which adults work full-time in the marketplace. Its demand for state-supported programs of day care discriminates against parents who choose to raise their own children and forces everyone to conform to the dominant pattern. Indifferent to this inequity, feminists extol the dominant pattern as the irresistible product of social developments analogous to the development of technology, which automatically renders old ways obsolete. The two-career family represents "progress," and laggards have to fall in line: Such is the logic feminists have borrowed from the marketplace without any awareness of its incompatibility with their vision of a kinder, gentler world.

Mainstream feminism is now concerned almost exclusively with a single goal—to "empower" women to enter business and the professions on an equal footing with men. Even its obsession with the abortion issue has to be seen in this light. Since the biology of reproduction is the most dramatic difference between men and women and the most important source, it appears, of women's industrial inequality, it is necessary to neutralize this "disability" by giving women absolute rights over the embryo. The assertion of "reproductive rights" removes the last obstacle to women's absorption into the work force. It is significant that the National Organization for Women (NOW) has failed to support legislation that would require employers to grant parental leaves. More flexible work schedules are not part of its agenda. Evidently because it believes that women would take advantage of such leaves more readily than would men, NOW suspects that a parental leave policy would perpetuate the division of labor that assigns women the primary role in child care and thus inhibits their professional advancement. In the highly competitive world of business and the professions, those who stray from the careerist path pay a heavy price. Advancement depends on an early start, a willingness to work long hours, and a single-minded adherence to the prevailing standards of productivity. Those who allow their children to slow them down lose out in the race for success.

A strategy more consistent with the original aims of the feminist movement, one might imagine, would challenge the prevailing definition of success. It would challenge the separation of the home and the workplace. It would criticize the suburban ideal, as it did in the beginning. It would criticize the re-creation of suburbia in the gentrified, yuppified city—another false solution that fails to address the real issue, the segregation of home life and work life. Without advocating a return to household production, a feminism worthy of the name would insist on a closer integration between people's professional lives and their domestic lives. Instead of acquiescing in the family's subordination to the workplace, it would seek to remodel the workplace around the needs of the family. It would question the ideology of economic growth and productivity, together with the careerism it fosters. A feminist movement that respected the achievements of women in the past would not disparage housework, motherhood, or unpaid civic and neighborly services. It would not make a paycheck the only symbol of accomplishment. It would demand a system of production for use rather than profit. It would insist that people need self-respecting, honorable callings, not glamorous careers that carry high salaries but take them away from their families. Instead of seeking to integrate women into the existing structures of the capitalist economy, it would appeal to women's issues in order to make the case for a complete transformation of those structures. It would reject not only the "feminine mystique" but the mystique of technological progress and economic development. It would no longer care about showing how "progressive" it was. By rejecting "progress," of course, it would put itself beyond the pale of respectable opinion—which is to say, it would become as radical as it now merely claims to be.

6

Gilligan's Island

Feminists have always found themselves torn between arguments that minimize the importance of sexual differences and arguments that run the risk of exaggerating them. Early campaigns for women's rights rested on the first of these strategies. The objection that civic equality would unsex women proved so effective, however, that feminists began to shift their ground. By the end of the nineteenth century, most of them had come to favor the claim that access to the ballot box and the professions would enlarge the domain of women's distinctive capacity for love and nurture. Once women gained access to the world of men, they argued, ruthless competition would give way to care and compassion.

An argument based on sexual differences has the advantage of linking feminism to a sweeping vision of social improvement. But it comes with a price. It tends to reaffirm the very stereotypes that have held women back. It seems to reinforce the social expectation that women will be soft and gentle, when they need to become tough-minded and assertive. Is it possible to have things both ways? Without reviving old habits of submission, to insist that women speak "in a different voice"?

Carol Gilligan has been struggling with this question throughout her career. *In a Different Voice*, published in 1982, was part of a new wave in feminist psychology, directed against theories of psychological development that (allegedly) equate maturity with individuation and separation and can thus interpret women's preference for connection and relatedness only as evidence of incomplete development. Much of this criticism was directed against Freud, who believed that "freedom consists of isolation," in the words of Jessica Benjamin, and that "denial of the need for the other" represents the only "route to independence."

Gilligan's primary target was not Freud but Lawrence Kohlberg, but she too objected to a "developmental litany," as she put it, that "intones the celebration of separation, autonomy, individuation, and natural rights." Since any deviation from this "masculine standard" could be dismissed as a "failure of development," the reigning psychological theories had the effect of giving scientific sanction to age-old beliefs about the inferiority of women. If women were judged by male standards, they would always come off looking second best. The only way to affirm women's equality, it appeared, was to insist on their difference.

Kohlberg traced moral reasoning through six distinct stages, culminating in respect for universal principles of justice such as the golden rule and the categorical imperative. The chief objection to his scheme is that it has so little to say about the conduct of life. Empty of substantive content, it does not tell us what is worth living or dying for. The principles Kohlberg wants us to honor are strictly procedural. They teach us to respect others' rights, but "the right" itself, according to Kohlberg, "is a matter of personal values and opinions." Kohlberg has no theory of goods as distinguished from rights. In effect, he makes toleration the test of moral growth, without explaining what ends toleration might serve beyond the preservation of a precarious social truce.

But Gilligan does not object to Kohlberg's theory because it is bland and noncommittal, or because it takes for granted the "relativism of personal values and opinions," or because it requires a "corresponding emphasis upon procedural rules for reaching consensus." She is Kohlberg's student as well as his critic. She too wants to promote cooperation and consensus. She appears to argue, however, that these ends are better served by a morality of caring and sharing than by a morality of rights and rules.

Gilligan accepts the conventional contrast between the "expressive" orientation of women and the "instrumental" orientation of men, but she resents the implication that concern for others, as opposed to a concern for abstract principles, signifies arrested development. Kohlberg saw only "conformity" in the idea that "good behavior is that which pleases or helps others." In his system, altruism represents a higher stage than egoism, but it still falls short of a morality that rests on abstract principles and procedures. Gilligan, on the other hand, distrusts abstract moral reasoning if it overrides the interpersonal context in which moral choices have to be made. Thus she refuses to see evidence of ethical immaturity in studies showing that girls will change the rules of a game in order to resolve disputes and "preserve relationships," in her words. The ability to nurture relationships, she thinks, is nothing to sneer at. If women speak a "distinct moral language" of their own, it is by no means a primitive dialect. Indeed, Gilligan gives the impression that it is a good deal more eloquent and expressive than the masculine dialect.

Her polemic against Kohlberg recalls the Romantic attack on instrumental reason, in which feeling was elevated above intellect, "feminine" mercy over "masculine" justice. It is the lingering influence of the Romantic tradition (evident once again in her *Meeting at the Crossroads: Women's Psychology and Girls' Development* (1992) in the form of an idealized view of childhood) that probably explains her readiness to embrace sexual stereotypes that might otherwise invite a great deal of skepticism. As the psychologist John M. Broughton has pointed out, interviews conducted by Gilligan herself show that women comfortably employ the "supposedly 'male' language of rights," while men often fall into the idiom of care and compassion. One male subject, asked to define morality, said that it was "not taking advantage of other people, not hurting them." Another, asked what obligations he felt toward others, replied: "To be honest with them, not to do anything which would hurt them." Gilligan's distinction between a "connected" and a "separate" sense of self comes out very clearly in an interview in which the subject refers to "being with other people and getting close to people" as the "most meaningful thing for myself right now." Unfortunately for Gilligan's hypothesis of a "different voice" in women, the speaker turns out to be a man.

Unembarrassed by such evidence, Gilligan insists that

"the male 'I' is defined in separation," and the feminine "I" in connection. She clings to this cliché even though it tends to encourage habits of self-effacement and submission in women. She herself recognizes the difficulty when she observes that women's gift for "caring" makes them reluctant to claim their rights. She agrees with Elizabeth Cady Stanton, to the point of reproducing Stanton's capital letters, that "SELF-DEVELOPMENT IS A HIGHER DUTY THAN SELF-SACRI-FICE."

Having rejected Kohlberg's scheme of development without calling into question its underlying model of moral development through sequential stages, Gilligan has to propose a new model for women that proceeds in the opposite direction, from altruism to egoism. Women, she seems to be saying, need to learn what men have to unlearn: a healthy regard for their own interests.

When she interviewed women referred to her study by an abortion clinic, she found that they rationalized abortion on the grounds that bearing a child would have been a selfish choice. It was a step forward, Gilligan argues, when they came to admit that abortion served their own wishes and needs. Not that abortion represents, for that reason, the selfish choice; as long as women share this "conventional interpretation" of the alternatives, they continue to vacillate between self-condemnation and transparent, unconvincing attempts at self-justification. Development, for women, means coming to see the "limitation of the opposition itself," which is "self-blinding" because it equates self-assertion with selfishness and thus encourages women to live exclusively for others. It is a sign of moral progress when Gilligan's subjects decided that "you can't worry about not hurting other people; just do what is right for you." Another woman in Gilligan's study, speaking of her earlier outlook on moral issues, summarizes the morality Gilligan wants women to outgrow: "I thought that as long as I didn't hurt anybody, everything would be fine."

Gilligan's revision of Kohlberg appears to leave us with a symmetrical pattern of development in which the two sexes proceed by different routes to the same place, a respect for abstract "human rights." Notwithstanding her objection to the concept of rights (which she often trivializes by reducing rights to rules), Gilligan cannot do without it. Women's emancipation remains for her what it was for so many earlier feminists, a matter of claiming their rights. That it is also a matter of doing away with double standards is a point that she chooses to ignore.

The effect of her analysis is to reassert double standards of competence, performance, and moral development while demanding respect for women's rights. Like Kohlberg, she gropes for a morality that transcends the conventional opposition between egoism and altruism. But she does not understand (any more than he does) that the only escape from the polarity of egoism and altruism lies in the selflessness experienced by those who lose themselves in their work, in the effort to master a craft or a body of knowledge, or in the acceptance of a formidable challenge that calls on all their resources. It is only in purposeful activity that we find a suspension of egoism that goes beyond conventional self-sacrifice.

For those who view ethical problems from a narrowly social point of view, people absorbed in their work appear self-absorbed and therefore suspicious. In fact they are blissfully self-forgetful; and although they may neglect their social duties, it can be argued that their self-respect makes them better citizens than all the selfless social service in the world. From this point of view, the reason women are so preoccupied with questions of selfishness and self-sacrifice is that they have historically enjoyed so few opportunities for challenging activity of an impersonal character. Having lacked those opportunities, many of them understandably lack the confidence to throw themselves into arduous, risky pursuits the mastery of which is the best recipe, perhaps the only recipe, for self-respect.

Gilligan wants women to respect themselves, but she cannot seem to see that self-respect comes from meeting impersonal standards. She subscribes (as her new book makes clear) to the current notion, widely shared by those who write about "self-esteem," that people come to grief when they try to live up to standards set by someone else. She can conceptualize self-respect only as the satisfaction of "doing what is right for you"—a nebulous formula that invites the suspicion of ordinary, old-fashioned selfishness (masked as "self-development"), unless "right for you" includes the effort to pit your talents against a demanding ideal of perfection. Since perfection, for Gilligan, is a snare and a delusion, her idea of self-respect remains stunted and deformed. All she sees in the ideal of perfection is the risk of failure and damaged "self-esteem."

In spite of her disagreements with Kohlberg, Gilligan tends to identify respect for "human rights," as he does, with the higher stages of moral development. Like Kohlberg, she confuses respect with tolerance and compassion, thereby inverting the meaning of respect, usually reserved for the acknowledgment of others' capacities and achievements. For Gilligan, respect implies no more than an acknowledgment of their weakness—their susceptibility to pain, their right not to be hurt. When she speaks of self-respect, she often seems to mean merely that a woman needs to "claim the right to include herself among the people whom she considers it moral not to hurt." Though she is eager to shed the discourse of egoism and altruism, the injunction against inflicting injury still provides Gilligan's moral touchstone. She urges only that women extend this injunction against injury to themselves. In this way, she hopes, they can assert their "human rights" without masculinizing themselves or equating femininity, on the other hand, with self-sacrifice.

In *A Different Voice*, Gilligan repeatedly speaks of the issue facing women—the issue raised by the difficulty of distinguishing "caring" and "relatedness" from self-sacrifice—as a "conflict between integrity and care." In her vocabulary, however, integrity does not mean what it usually means. It serves her simply as a slogan, a synonym for the self-assertion that women lack. She invokes integrity again and again but seems indifferent to its connotations of honesty and courage. Integrity refers, above all, to the courage of your convictions. It describes Luther at the Diet of Worms: "I neither can nor will revoke anything, seeing that it is not safe or right to act against conscience." It describes Joan of Arc confronting her accusers (in Shaw's telling): "What God made me do I will never go back on; and what He has commanded or shall command I will not fail to do in spite of any man alive." At a less exalted level of moral heroism, it describes the refusal to give in to the line of least resistance, to follow the crowd, or to court popularity at the price of honesty and self-respect. This virtue, it should be added, has no gender. Men are no more exempt than women from the temptation to trim their sails to the wind; no more likely, therefore, to make integrity a way of life. Loyalty to a principle, a cause, or an idea—to the inner promptings of conscience—does not come any more easily to men than to women.

Pressures to conform are even stronger in the case of women, to be sure; and Gilligan's new book, although it does not explain them satisfactorily, provides a vivid picture of just how intense those pressures can be. Written in collaboration with Lyn Mikel Brown and with the support of a team of researchers, *Meeting at the Crossroads* rests on a five-year study of a private day school for girls, specifically on interviews with 100 girls between the ages of 7 and 18. Impressed with Gilligan's initial finding that women speak a moral language of their own, she and her colleagues decided to extend their research "further back into girls' childhood" in the hope of unraveling the "mystery in girls' development."

They visited a variety of schools and published selected interviews from time to time. In the course of the research leading to the present study, they became increasingly dissatisfied with "standard practices of psychological research," which put the girls on their guard and inhibited a "real relationship" between the research team and its subjects. When the researchers encouraged the girls to speak more freely, they found themselves "face to face with difficult questions of truthfulness and authenticity in relationships between girls and women." They found, in other words, that girls too often say what they think adults want to hear—especially, it might be added, when they are being interviewed. Conformity to adult expectations, they decided, explained why "lively," "outspoken" girls become increasingly timid as adolescents, lose confidence in themselves, suppress their own opinions, "pretend things are fine," and "smile all the time" in the hope of making themselves agreeable.

Here again Gilligan's data often seem to be at odds with her conclusions. She and Brown deplore the "self-silencing" that sustains a "patina of niceness and piety," but the impression conveyed by their description of school life is a good deal more grim than these words would suggest. Niceness and piety are not much in evidence at Laurel School in

Cleveland. The social tone, moreover, is set not by adults, but by adolescent cliques and clubs with their gossip, their whispered secrets, and their rigorously enforced structure of popularity. The girl who establishes herself as a social arbiter among her classmates "takes them into her group," as one of them astutely observes, "and teaches them not to like certain people." The competition for status takes a heavy toll even on those who succeed. Believing that "it's not good to hurt someone," these girls can see all too clearly that popularity requires them to hurt people and that in most situations, therefore, someone will "feel bad, whichever decision I make." Those who refuse or fail to ingratiate themselves with the dominant cliques—the "leftovers," as one of them calls herself—become prematurely jaded and cynical, convinced that "the only person you can rely on is yourself."

Gilligan's early work celebrated women's "concern with relationships" as the source of their "morality of responsibility"; but the snobbery and the backbiting that prevail at Laurel School might well give her pause about the "human strength" of "affiliative ways of living." The ugly side of adolescent sociability suggests that a "web of relationships" can be suffocating, inhibiting, and oppressive rather than "creative and cooperative." A dawning awareness of this may help to account for Gilligan's occasional uneasiness, never clearly explained or absorbed into the structure of her analysis, with the sexual stereotypes that figured so prominently in *A Different Voice* and continue to reverberate in *Crossroads*.

She and Brown observe in passing that it seems "profoundly misleading" to describe women as "connected" and men as "separate." Such characterizations, they say, ignore the "depths of men's desire for relationship and the anger women feel about not having power in the world." But this is a trivial objection. They would have done better to remind themselves, on the strength of their own evidence, that women are just as likely as men to misuse power, to relish cruelty, and to indulge the taste for cruelty in enforcing conformity. Study of a girls' school would seem to provide the ideal corrective to sentimental views of women's natural gift for nurture and compassion. "Those who have experienced dismissal by the junior high school girls' clique," writes Elizabeth Fox-Geno-vese, "could hardly, with a straight face, claim generosity and nurture as a natural attribute of women."

Brown and Gilligan would be uncomfortable, I suspect, with the suggestion that women and men are equals in their capacity not only for kindness but for cruelty. It is an article of faith, among those who claim to speak for the oppressed and exploited, that black people, say, cannot be accused of racism or that women should not be judged by "masculine" standards of justice. Early feminists refused to absolve their sisters in this way. Indeed they were sometimes accused of hating women, because they dwelled unsparingly on the petty tyrannies by means of which women sought to compensate themselves for the narrowness of their lives.

The demand for access to the great world of politics and learning derived its original force from the observation that narrow circumstances breed narrow minds. But when feminists began to argue for their rights on the grounds that it would give "maternal influence" a wider sphere, they sacrificed moral realism to political expediency. They turned conventional stereotypes to political advantage but lost the ability to explain what makes the world of women, unless it is integrated into a more impersonal world where the quality of ideas or workmanship counts for more than "relationships," so confining to the spirit, so productive of petty jealousies, so highly charged with envy and resentment.

In seeking to explain why adolescents lose the candor and

the independence of girlhood, Gilligan and Brown ignore the tyranny exercised by those who control social eligibility and exclusion. They believe that if adolescents learn "to cover over their own feelings and hide what they know," it is because they have internalized the false ideal of femininity held up by a patriarchal culture. Adopting the "narrowing visions of nice and kind women" held up to them by their elders, they replace their own voices with the "foreign voice-overs of adults." "Injunctions to be nice," according to Gilligan and Brown, reduce high-spirited girls to young ladies, the epitome of propriety and decorum. "Culturally inscribed and socially institutionalized notions of womanhood" win out over "authenticity." The "strengths in girls' voices" become inaudible, silenced by "accepted norms of female behavior."

This explanation seems implausible on the face of it, in view of the intense competition for status that makes school life so harrowing for many girls—a competition in which "niceness" has very little relation to success. It is doubly implausible, this talk of decorous womanhood, in view of the inescapable influence of competing models of womanhood. The girls at Laurel School are not so completely isolated from the world around them, presumably, that they have escaped exposure to a feminism that challenges "accepted norms of behavior" at every point. If accepted norms of any kind can still be said to exist, they are probably shaped more directly by feminism than by the old ideal of feminine submission.

We should take care, however, not to exaggerate the influence of adult ideals, feminist or otherwise, on the con-temporary subculture of adolescents. We should take partic-ular care not to fall into a familiar idealization of the young, according to which the corrupting influence of the adult world gradually prevails over the spontaneity and charm of childhood. A long tradition, dating back to Rousseau, glorifies children as noble savages, unspoiled by adult inhibitions and self-censorship. A variant of this tradition, in fiction and folklore, takes the part of the tomboy against the social constraints conspiring to make her into a proper young lady. *Meeting at the Crossroads* takes some of its resonance from this genre. It tells a story many readers will dimly recall, in which prepubescent girls, enterprising and "psychologically astute," enjoy "genuine or authentic" relationships to those around them but are gradually forced to adopt the ways of civilization, betrayed by an "image of the perfectly nice and caring girl."

Gilligan and Brown read the annals of Laurel, then, as another chapter in the "conflict between integrity and care," with a subplot that vaguely alludes to *Little Women*, *The Secret Garden*, and other classic tales of enterprising girlhood. But the absence of adult ideals, not their ruthless imposition, is the real story here. The girls at Laurel suffer from the effects of generational segregation, the deflation of ideals, the loss of an impersonal public order. In most societies known to historians or to anthropologists, the young get an education by working alongside adults. The requirement that adolescents spend most of their time in school is a fairly recent innovation, closely linked to the rise of modern nation-states.

Formal schooling prolongs adolescence, and at the same time walls it off from unsupervised, pedagogically unmediated contact with the world of adults. Fortunately, schools are never wholly self-contained. Adolescents avid for knowledge of the world have always managed to evade pedagogical supervision and to acquire vicarious experience of adult ways, largely through the medium of unauthorized reading. Educational practice, moreover, is often inconsistent and contradictory. On the one hand, it seeks to discourage independent exploration on the part of the young. On the other hand, its attempts to inculcate "Americanism" through exposure to patriotic narratives—an important objective of schooling in the days before patriotism became suspect—tend to stimulate forms of curiosity about the past, about the realm of affairs and adventure, that easily escape pedagogical control.

It is only in our own time that schools have fully committed themselves to the dogma of immediacy, to the deadly notion that young people can be interested only in things directly touching their own lives. The replacement of historical narratives by the study of "social problems," the preference for literary works with a contemporary setting and an adolescent cast of characters, and the attempt to sanitize the curriculum by eliminating anything that might give offense all serve to discourage imaginative identification with images of the exotic or unfamiliar. Adolescents will not get much sense of a life beyond adolescence from a reading list limited to *Lord of the Flies, To Kill a Mockingbird,* and *The Catcher in the Rye.*

The girls at Laurel pay dearly for their isolation from the great world. Their idea of freedom is to "go somewhere of my own choice—like to Burger King or Wendy's." Their idea of education is "to get into college, and that's the only reason I'm here." Their vocabulary is pathetically reduced, their speech halting and clumsy. "I was like screaming on the phone. . . . I was like, 'I don't care,' you know." "She's like, 'I'm going to kill myself,' and I'm like, 'Don't kill yourself until morning, I'm really tired.' " "I saw them, and it's like, 'Oh, wow!' You know." "I decided I'd say yes and explain because that would be like the best thing to do." "Like everybody hates her in class." "You can't survive like alone, you can't like sit on a mountain and be alone." "Like if you are, I don't know, if you're sort of like thrown together with someone you try to like adapt to them, so I don't know."

These girls lack any sense of an impersonal order that exists independently of their wishes and anxieties. Not only the substance but also the manner of their speech testify to the emptiness and unreality of a life that consists only of "relationships." The compulsive "like" conveys a disbelief in the objective reality of their surroundings. It blurs every boundary, retracts every assertion, and thus serves notice that the speaker is not to be held accountable for anything she says.

It would be a great mistake to jump to the conclusion that, because these girls are inarticulate, because their troubles are trivial on the scale of the world's troubles, and because most of them "have access to many of the privileges which this society offers those who are born into favorable conditions," as Brown and Gilligan delicately put it, their anguish is negligible or unreal. Their anguish is palpable, even though they cannot find words to express it. It derives from the same condition that makes them tongue-tied: the absence of impersonal aspirations, impersonal standards of comparison that would give their lives an element of continuity and shelter them from the vicissitudes of "relationships." Lacking any larger frame of reference, they invest all their emotions in the competition for acceptance by their peers. Social approval inevitably proves too precarious to carry such a heavy load. Friendships can hardly flourish when "you have to like keep your eyes open at all times." Self-protection becomes the overriding imperative.

Gilligan and Brown deplore the "standards of perfection" held up to girls by their elders. Laurel's malady, they insist, is the "seduction of the unattainable." Therapeutic criticism of standards and ideals, however, will only aggravate the condition they wish to cure. The same thing goes for the feminist assault on history as "his story," the assault on literary culture as a culture of dead white European males. Earlier feminists demanded admission to the republic of letters, but today many of them counsel a retreat into a world of women.

In the course of their work at Laurel, Brown and Gilligan organized a series of retreats, at which teachers and researchers agonized about the "absence of authentic communication" between girls and women. It never occurred to the participants to ask whether the students were getting anything for their minds to work on, anything that might set fire to the imagination, anything that might take them out of themselves. The teachers readily accepted the researchers' contention that they themselves, as one of the teachers said, "provided the models for . . . behaving like 'good little girls.' " Having confessed their crimes, they commended the research team for bringing them all together. Everybody agreed that "the sanctuary of a retreat setting allowed us to understand our knowledge and feelings with a clarity not possible in hierarchical work settings." They "wept."

At one point, the teachers were shocked to hear that some of the girls at Laurel preferred to be taught by men, who "treat us like people" and "bring themselves into their teaching." They might have asked themselves just what it was that men brought to the classroom. The suggestion of a larger world? The hint of things undreamed of in Laurel's therapeutic philosophy? The exercise of impersonal authority? Instead the teachers and researchers asked themselves, all over again, why it was so difficult for girls and women to establish a "genuine relationship." The moment of reckoning passed, the circle of women closed again, the danger of illumination receded. The talk ended where it began. It ended, that is—as it will always end if women choose to retreat into a little world of their own—with a renewed commitment to openness, authenticity, cooperation, compassion, and care.

7

The Mismeasure of Man

Havelock Ellis once warned V. F. Calverton, who proposed to write a history of women in several volumes, that the subject would defeat anyone who tried to do justice to its scope and complexity. The history of women could not be detached from the history of the human race in general, Ellis said, without reducing it to something "slight & superficial & secondhand." A serious history of women would become a history of intimacy—"a history of mankind in a more intimate sense than anything yet attempted." "It would require an enormously long period of preliminary preparation, a knowledge of many sciences and a familiarity with many languages." His own *Studies in the Psychology of Sex*, he pointed out, had consumed more than twenty years, while James Frazer had given up a whole lifetime to *The Golden Bough*, living the "life of a recluse" and sacrificing "nearly all other interests"; and the history of women, which raised questions "perhaps rather similar" to the ones Frazer had wrestled with, was a much larger subject than either of these others. Calverton's "five to ten volumes" would barely scratch the surface. A "serious writer" ought to "hesitate a very, very long time" before setting off on a journey that would prove endless.

Many years of inconclusive struggle with the subject that Calverton had the sense to abandon have taught me, rather belatedly, the wisdom of Ellis's cautionary words; nor has the rise of "gender studies" offered much in the way of offsetting encouragement. I do not mean to deny that we have learned a great deal in the last thirty years about the history of feminism, the history of women's work, the history of marriage and the family, even the history of love. But the history of women itself—the history that can't be captured by a "strictly ethnographical" approach or "limited to the bald facts," as Ellis put it—remains elusive.

As scholarly attention shifts from the record of women's activity to the "social construction of gender," that history becomes more elusive than ever. Much of the recent work in the field seems only to belabor the obvious: that the cultural definition of womanhood has undergone many changes over time; that these changes ought to make us wary of statements claiming to define women's essential nature; and nevertheless that "gender seems to be a stubbornly ubiquitous feature of culture," in the words of Christine DiStefano, even if we no longer have much confidence in our ability to describe it.

The current outcry against "essentialism" has not discouraged feminist scholars from efforts to explain what makes women different from men. But the effort seems largely misplaced. If the difference is rooted in biology, then it has no history. If it is the product of inequities that have forced women to cultivate the vices and virtues of the downtrodden, then the history of gender tends to dissolve into a monotonous story of oppression relieved only by occasional "subversions" of patriarchal authority. The history of women's activity, of course, is another matter. The record of what women have actually done and said, not necessarily in their capacity as women but in their capacity as workers and writers, adds immeasurably to historical understanding. It does nothing, however, to unlock the mystery of gender.

The same difficulties confront those who now attempt to write the history of masculinity. Books on this subject, most of them flagrantly imitative of similar books on women, are rolling off the presses at a rapid pace. Feminists, who initially resisted "men's studies" as an infringement of their own domain, an attempt to present the oppressor as a victim in his own right, have apparently decided that explorations of masculinity are ideologically acceptable, since they almost invariably "debunk the Marlboro man," as the *Chronicle of Higher Education* reports approvingly. The *Chronicle* lists twenty-eight recent and forthcoming books on men and masculinity and leaves us with the sinking feeling that this is only the beginning. The market for self-pity, it appears, is inexhaustible.

Even at their best, it is hard to see how books in this vein can avoid the difficulties already evident in work on the construction of femininity. Kevin White's contribution, *The First Sexual Revolution* (1993), which bears an imposing subtitle promising to trace the "emergence of male heterosexuality in modern America," turns out to be a study of the liberalization of sexual morality that took place in the '20s and '30s—a subject long familiar to historians as the "revolution in manners and morals." White seems to have grown more and more skeptical about gender studies as he went along. By the end of the book, he has pretty well decided that "the dynamics of sex and gender alone cannot explain the construction of power in personal life." The "mere study of gender," he says, "may be a red herring in the search to improve human social relations" or to understand the past. True enough; but in that case, what is the point of a book about the "construction of masculinity"?

In *American Manhood: Transformations in Masculinity from the Revolution to the Modern Era* (1993) E. Anthony Rotundo is untroubled by such doubts, although he takes pains to distinguish his approach from that of the "mythopoetic men's movement" led by Robert Bly. He condemns Bly's "essentialism," which assumes that "manhood begins with a timeless, unchanging core of qualities that all men ultimately possess." His own stance, Rotundo wants us to know, is "one of 'cultural construction': manhood is a mental category created and re-created by cultures as they . . . change." Founded on a cliché, his argument contains no surprises. The explanatory framework is familiar, even trite. In the nineteenth century, the story goes (and Rotundo's study is limited to this century, notwithstanding another expansive set of titles), American culture's center of gravity shifted from the community to the individual, and the masculine role came to emphasize careers rather than the responsibilities of a head of the household. The doctrine of "separate spheres" for men and women—another theme made familiar by historians mainly concerned with the lives of women—left women in charge of the family, while men turned their attention to the larger world outside.

Haunted by the danger of being "lured back into women's sphere," they became workaholics and overachievers. The fear of softness, Rotundo insists, grew increasingly troublesome as the nineteenth century drew to a close, partly because men now felt threatened by feminism. They threw themselves into competitive sports and cultivated "primitive" virtues as an antidote to the "overcivilized" habits widely deplored by turn-of-the-century commentators on American life. The word "sissy" entered the language, as a description of everything that men were afraid of becoming. "Confused and defensive," the American male "needed to prove himself a man." This compulsion to be tough, this "turning away from women," has continued to define masculinity, according to Rotundo. A ten-page epilogue, "Manhood in the Twentieth Century," leaves the impression that nothing has changed during the last 100 years: a revealing instance of the flattening effect encouraged by gender studies.

Or is it simply Rotundo's lack of imagination that accounts for the weaknesses of this book—not so much the conceptual framework imposed by gender as the hamhanded way in which he proceeds to deck it out? The subject demands a light touch, a good ear and a sensitivity to subtle shades of meaning—attributes with which Rotundo is not abundantly endowed. He lacks all sense of irony. When a woman wittily refers to the "elemental simplicity of the average masculine mind" in an article in *Harper's Bazaar,* he takes the remark at face value and adds the ponderous explanation that "a new concept of manly reason was emerging here." He reads *The Bostonians,* in which Henry James subjected both feminism and anti-feminism to a deftly satirical treatment, as if the protagonist's fulminations against a "womanized age" expressed James's own opinions. He makes the same mistake when he comes across a book called *Haven in a Heartless*

World—the "best example," he says, of historians' sentimentalization of nineteenth-century family life, even though the title refers not to the author's view of the family but precisely to the view he seeks to refute.

To blame the notion of gender for such egregious misreadings might seem a little unjust; gender studies, it might be argued, are the victim, and not the villain, of this particular exercise in historical simplification. Still, gender provides a context in which this kind of misreading is likely to occur. Take Rotundo's muddled discussion of the "strenuous life" promoted by Theodore Roosevelt, Oliver Wendell Holmes and others. These men were more alarmed by the declining influence of their class than by threats to their masculinity. As they saw it, men of breeding and family were being shoved aside by unscrupulous spoilsmen and self-made tycoons. Instead of contesting control of the nation's political and financial institutions, the genteel classes were retreating to the sidelines, cultivating an air of amused or indignant detachment.

Roosevelt wanted his class to toughen itself without losing its decency or its commitment to fair play. He called for the "virtue that shall be strong." Rotundo, noting Roosevelt's enthusiasm for manly sports—"gentlemanly contests for supremacy" on the gridiron—misses the force of his adjective. Roosevelt's program aimed to produce gentlemen, not roughnecks and he-men. Similar concerns informed the movement for "muscular Christianity," another attempt to reinvigorate the forces of decency. Rotundo's focus on gender captures only the muscles, blurring the Christianity they were meant to serve.

In the two or three decades before the First World War, the air was full of misgivings, not by any means invariably linked to the decline of Christianity or to the abdication of the old Protestant elites, about the deadening effects of industrial civilization. Life seemed too highly organized, too self-conscious, too predictable to allow for the unpremeditated play of impulse. Industrialism had reduced everything to a routine. The material comforts it provided made people increasingly averse to risky pursuits; they shied away from anything that might disturb their safety or their peace of mind. Science enhanced human control over nature, but it left human beings more fearful than ever of what could not be controlled. Instead of opening up larger possibilities, science appeared to shrink the scope of human aspiration. People were afraid to venture out of the narrow circle of its protection. Dependent on technologies they no longer understood, they were incompetent to manage even the exigencies of daily life. Even their amusements were mass produced. Not only the capacity for bold action, but everyday self-reliance, once the hallmark of American character, seemed to have given way to reliance on organized systems of production, distribution and expertise.

William James touched a raw nerve when he spoke of the spiritual "desiccation" that afflicted the modern world. The apprehensions that became fully articulate in his famous essay "The Moral Equivalent of War"—an argument against war that nevertheless recognized "martial virtues" as "absolute and permanent human goods"—cannot be dismissed as the lamentations of a dying class, let alone as a panicky male reaction to the rise of feminism. To diminish them in this way diminishes all of us—not just the historical actors whose motives Rotundo has reduced to the crudest terms, but also his readers, who are made to feel superior, in their current state of sexual enlightenment, to those who allegedly subscribed to stereotypical views of masculinity in the unenlightened past. If this gratuitous sense of superiority is the best that gender studies can offer, we can probably get along without them.

"The study of gender," Rotundo says, "has been derided as . . . an intellectual plaything of feminists which would drop from consideration if not for their political pressure." His book aims "to correct this dismissive attitude." It is more likely to have the opposite effect. A preoccupation with gender, if this example of the genre is any indication, tends to coarsen our sensibilities rather than to refine them. It replaces historical explanation with formulas, rips ideas out of context and often strengthens the very stereotypes it seeks to discredit. It divides the world along a single axis, leaving the impression that every form of conflict can be reduced to the opposition between men and women. Thus Rotundo refers to the nineteenth-century politics of feminism and anti-feminism as if these positions coincided with the categories of gender. "It is no wonder," he writes, ". . . that men opposed women's suffrage so fiercely," forgetting that many of them favored it and that many women, moreover, did not.

Yet Rotundo himself presents a good deal of evidence, in passing, that points to a different and more interesting interpretation not only of the feminist controversy, but of the widespread criticism of "desiccation." In a chapter on "boy culture," he shows that middle-class boys in the nineteenth century spent a large part of the time in a world of their own, "surprisingly free of adult supervision." They invented their own games and rituals, challenged each other to spontaneous feats of daring and agility, acted out stories of heroic adventure and collaborated in the enforcement of an informal code of honor that stressed courage, loyalty and stoic endurance of pain.

Boyhood patterns of self-directed activity persisted into young adulthood, as Rotundo shows in suggestive chapters on "male youth culture" and "male intimacy." Unmarried men conducted a large part of their education without any direction from adults. They organized debating societies and "library associations," which combined intellectual combat with festivity. "The ceaseless clash of wits between friends recalled the physical combat of loyal playfellows in boyhood," Rotundo writes. "Although the means of expression changed, the basic principle of mixing affection with attack remained the same."

Informal associations devoted to collective self-culture served young men as a "substitute for college," as one of them put it. These societies maintained their own libraries, sponsored lectures and gave their members a chance to test their learning in theatricals or debates. College fraternities provided another setting for activities that enlisted sociability in the service of self-improvement. "We educated each other," one man recalled, "by criticizing and laughing at each other."

By the end of the century, autonomous organizations of young men had either disappeared or degenerated into drinking and eating clubs. Education was increasingly confined to the classroom, agonistic rivalry to the playing field. Formal pedagogy replaced spontaneous play and self-culture. It was not the growing stress on competition that distinguished organized athletics from the informal games of an earlier time, as Rotundo argues, but the subordination of play to purposes dictated by adults. The expansion of extracurricular activities, at every level of the school system, reflected the expansion of pedagogical authority over young people formerly left to their own devices. The dead hand of the educator reached deep into childhood, redesigning life as a "learning experience."

The pedagogical invasion of childhood and youth was only one instance of a more general campaign to subject formerly unsupervised activities to systematic study and control. The same impulse found expression in efforts to systematize housekeeping and child-rearing, to penetrate the "conspiracy of silence" surrounding sex and to gain access to the inner life through methods ranging from mind-cure techniques to the most sophisticated psychologies. The institutionalization of new sciences and pseudo-sciences—home economics, sexology, social work, psychoanalysis, child development, the "science" of pedagogy—reflected an attempt to apply to everyday life the same administrative techniques that had been applied so successfully to the market and the state.

The "colonization of the life-world," as Jürgen Habermas calls it, meant that nothing was to be exempt from pedagogical or therapeutic mediation. Informal, customary and morally regulated conduct was to be organized on a new basis and administered by experts equipped with the latest technologies of the self. If the "life-world" represents the "totality of what is taken for granted," in the words of Alfred Schutz and Thomas Luckmann, then the determination to take nothing for granted, least of all the "socialization" of the young, exposed it to the steady encroachment of organized expertise in the irresistible form of money and power.

These developments undeniably expanded the horizon of human understanding and fostered a critical spirit, but in everyday life they were more likely to be experienced as a subjection to routines that drained the joy out of work and play and wrapped everything in a smothering self-consciousness. Surely it was this feeling of suffocation, much more than the need to prove something about masculinity, that explains the idealization of the strenuous life at the turn of the century: the attraction of imperialism and war, the longing for wide-open spaces, the new interest in the primitive and exotic, the nostalgia for simplicity and lost innocence.

Men were not alone, after all, in their dissatisfaction with a social order in which everything was organized down to the last detail. The rationalization of daily life had similarly depressing effects on women, even though it was often held up as the means of their emancipation from domestic drudgery. Much of the opposition to feminism derived from the perception that it had allied itself too closely with demands for the collectivization of housework and child-rearing and with the "repeal of reticence," in Agnes Repplier's memorable phrase. A convent-educated Philadelphia Catholic and prolific author of essays now regrettably forgotten, Repplier objected to the rage for sexual disclosure, specifically to the movement for sex education, on the grounds that "vital facts, the great laws of propagation," were "matters of casual concern" to children. Her account of her own childhood evoked a world full of activity and incident, to which adult concerns were decidedly peripheral—a world not so different from the old-fashioned "boy culture" described by Rotundo:

> A child's life is so full, and everything that enters it seems of supreme importance. I fidgeted over my hair which would not curl. I worried over my examples which never came out right. . . . I imagined I was stolen by brigands, and became—by virtue of beauty and intelligence—spouse of a patriotic outlaw in a frontier-less land. I asked artless questions. . . . But how could we fidget over obstetrics when we were learning to skate, and our very dreams were a medley of ice and bumps? How could we worry over "natural laws" in the face of a tyrannical interdict which lessened our chances of breaking our necks by forbidding us to coast down a hill covered with trees?

The ascendancy of experts, with their demand that children be exposed to "crude, undigested knowledge, without limit and without reserve," seemed to Repplier to threaten childhood with extinction.

Some of the material in Kevin White's book can be read as further evidence of the discontents attendant on the colonization of everyday life. In the 1920s, White argues, middle-class men began to look for models of spontaneous, uninhibited vitality in the subterranean subcultures that flourished on the margins of respectable society. Writers like Sherwood Anderson, Carl Van Vechten and Waldo Frank discovered in the ghetto an "unconscious love of inanimate things lost to the whites," as Anderson put it—"skies, the river, a moving boat—black mysticism." Frank described black men as "big fellows with flourishing mustaches, bushy brows." He admired their "obscene" and "brutal energy."

Tramps and vagabonds commended themselves to a number of writers for the same reason. In their voluntary exile, tramps lived dangerously, mocked convention and treated women with a casual contempt that women allegedly found irresistible. Harry Kemp, whose *Tramping on Life* later inspired Jack Kerouac's *On the Road*, delighted in a young woman's "shrill exclamation of virginal fright, not at me,— but at my abrupt, hungry masculinity." Bernarr Macfadden's pulp magazine *True Story* popularized images of men who took what they wanted without waiting for anyone's permission. The Christian gentleman, White observes, no longer stood as the model of American manhood. A mixture of bohemian and proletarian influences contributed to his decline. "Middle-class men were infatuated with working-class [that is, *lumpenproletarian*] sexuality."

White does not explain why the most "advanced" ideas so often inclined toward the primitive; he is content to deplore the rise of "underworld primitivism at the expense of gentlemanliness." It would be hard to quarrel with his contention, drawn from case studies of marital experiments ostensibly based on sexual equality, that men who admired the freedom of the lower orders, as they imagined it, tended to equate feminism with "varietism"—unrestricted license for both partners, with no questions asked. Unions based on these notions almost invariably came to grief. Egalitarian unions worked best, according to White, when they were monogamous and otherwise quite conventional. What needs to be explained, however, is the persistent feeling that something was missing even from a well-regulated, sexually emancipated life conducted according to impeccably egalitarian principles—indeed, that this kind of life in some deeper sense was not worth living.

This feeling is easy to ridicule, especially when it issues in an ideology of red-blooded manhood. As Bly admits in his much-abused best seller *Iron John*, the myth of the "Wild Man"—the uses of which, he argues, have been forgotten in a rationalized, disenchanted world—sounds like a "silly phrase when we first hear it," another name for "irresponsible man or churlish man." To both White and Rotundo, it sounds not only silly but dangerous. "The '90s have seen an attempt to rediscover men's primitive roots," White says, citing Bly; but "a regression toward more primitivism surely is not a solution." Bly's celebration of the warrior ideal, according to Rotundo, has "striking parallels" with the "movement toward primitive masculinity at the turn of the twentieth century."

But Bly's rehabilitation of "mythological thinking" should not be confused with a "monotonously aggressive" mode of masculinity, which he expressly condemns. The cult of toughness and the cult of sensitivity, as Bly sees them, are two sides of the same coin. Both originate in the absence of male authority over boys and young men. If the soft and sensitive male, more attuned to women's suffering than to his own, has failed to make a "clean break with the mother," the predatory male severs the connection only by suppressing the tender feelings that come to be identified, in a culture in which the nurturing side of fatherhood is so little in evidence, exclusively with women. "There's a general assumption now," Bly says, "that every man in a position of power is . . . corrupt and oppressive." It is taken for granted, moreover, that women know more about "relationships" than men. When adult manhood labors under such a heavy cloud of suspicion, young men have to choose between equally unsatisfactory alternatives: to become more like women or to embrace a masculine style that leaves no room for love and friendship with members of either sex.

None of this is nearly so threatening or outrageous as it has been made out to be by Bly's detractors, most of whom have obviously not bothered to read what he has written. What he says about the eclipse of fatherhood and its effects finds ample confirmation in the sociological and psychoanalytic literature. His readings of myths and fairy tales are sensible and persuasive. If the men's "movement" nevertheless seems a little ridiculous, it is not because Bly calls for a reassertion of heroism, because he insists that young men can be initiated into manhood only by adult males or because he refuses to concede the "moral high ground" to those who urge us just to "be human, and not talk about masculine or feminine at all." It is because he offers his reinterpretation of mythology not just as a metaphorical elaboration of enduring moral insights but as a program, an answer to the contemporary malaise. He offers it, in a manner reminiscent of Jung, as a cure for souls, a world-saving therapy for those who no longer believe in religion but appreciate the power and beauty of ancient myths.

But aesthetic appreciation, alas, cannot take the place of an authoritative spiritual discipline. Nor can mythology mean for us what it meant to those who took it as literal truth. The critical elucidation that makes it accessible to us simultaneously destroys its value as a guide to conduct. We cannot think ourselves into a state of mind in which the meaning of masculinity and femininity is palpable and unambiguous. In the mythological imagination, these distinctions appeared to be anchored in the eternal order of things. For us, they have become deeply problematic. The controversy about their meaning and significance, which shows no signs of abating, cannot be resolved by an appeal to the inner structure of the universe. We have to appeal instead to the evidence of anthropology, biology, history, psychology and of course to the evidence of mythology as well, for what it reveals not about the structure of the universe but about the human imagination. "Masculine" and "feminine" belong to the growing body of ideas that can no longer be taken for granted.

For that very reason, however, gender studies misrepresent the past when they attribute to our predecessors our own confusion and uncertainty about these matters. The problem for historical study is when and where and for what reasons gender has become an issue. To make it the central theme of history creates the impression that it has been an issue everywhere at all times—the overriding issue, in fact. But gender, like happy families, has no history. It emerges into history only at those moments when it becomes critically conscious of itself. The history of gender, if it aspires to something more than truisms, can only refer to the controversy about gender, which varies in intensity from time to time and from one place to another. For reasons that are important to explore, that controversy has reached a new peak of intensity in recent years. But the passion with which it is debated makes it all the more important to remember that people, even now, are likely to have a great many other things on their minds besides the battle of the sexes.

8

Misreading the Facts about Families

In her book *Brave New Families: Stories of Domestic Upheaval in Late Twentieth Century America* (1990) Judith Stacey wants to convince us that feminism is not a movement of upper-middle-class women alone and that working-class women, indeed, are the "genuine postmodern family pioneers." The "diversity and the innovative character of many working-class kin relationships"—the prevalence of extended families, blended families, and single-parent households—belie the "Archie Bunker" stereotype, according to Stacey. Wrongly condemned (or celebrated) as "profamily reactionaries," working-class women have shouldered the "burdens of freedom" and begun to devise "creative strategies" for dealing with the collapse of the nuclear family. Even if they do not always identify themselves as feminists, they have absorbed feminist ideas and are experimenting with "alternative models of femininity." Their success in "actively remaking family life" should reassure those who have been taken in by the "popular lament over family decline." The "modern" family may be declining (since it is no longer possible for most husbands to support a wife who stays at home with the children), but the "postmodern," "recombinant" family that is taking its place is a more democratic institution, far more deserving of our support.

On the face of it, Stacey's research does not lend much support to these cheery conclusions. Her resistance to the implications of her own evidence—her determination to rescue from the evidence support for the ideological preconceptions with which she began—is the real story here, more exciting than "stories of domestic upheaval." She studied two women in Silicon Valley, their families, and their friends. One of these women had to cope with divorce, a rocky second marriage, and three difficult children with marital troubles of their own. The other endured a whole series of calamities. Her violent marriage several times approached the point of collapse until it ended, after a reconciliation, in the untimely death of her husband. Her eldest son died in an auto crash; the youngest is a drug addict and dealer who has spent a good deal of time in jail. One of her three daughters attempted suicide after she discovered that her husband, a heavy drug-user, alcoholic, and part-time criminal by whom she had four children in rapid succession, was seeing another woman. She died of cancer in her twenties. Another daughter, a high school dropout, became an unwed mother at an early age, married and divorced another man who beat her (as her father had beaten her mother), and separated from her second husband—an amiable but lazy fellow (a "postfeminist man," in Stacey's euphemistic formulation) who was quite happy to stay home while she supported the family—when he tried to undermine her son's faith in God.

As Stacey writes, "most of the Lewisons lived hard, drove fast, spent impulsively, and partook liberally of high-risk diets, tobacco, alcohol, and often, drugs. Their leisure time preferences—gambling, flirting, racing, shooting—reflected and reinforced the provocative and ambivalent character of their relationship to social stability." In plain English, these people live on the edge. They exemplify, in exaggerated form, the impulsive and self-destructive tendencies that are always present in working-class life: an inability or refusal to plan ahead or save or hold a steady job; a fatalism that often seems to go hand-in-hand with a desperate need to tempt fate, to face it down; hot-tempered violence; ill-advised sexual attractions that dissolve in recriminations; and all the other habits that have always horrified middle-class observers of working-class culture.

People like the Lewisons find a steadying influence— insofar as they find anything to cling to at all—in the extended family (even though family connections are at the same time an endless source of conflict) and in the church. Both of the principal women in Stacey's book are fundamentalist Christians, as are many other members of both families. It says a great deal about the role of religion in these people's lives that the Lewisons left the Universal Temple of the Spirit, an unconventional, nondenominational sect, and returned to their Methodist congregation when the minister of the Universal Temple failed to show enough appreciation of the family's grief over the death of their son. The Lewisons look to the church for comfort, and they have no patience with churches that fail to provide it.

The exuberance and pathos of working-class culture, on the margins where the wish for respectability is repeatedly thwarted and finally almost extinguished both by circumstances and by reckless, willful invitations to disaster, are a familiar story, as are the mingled warmth and frustration experienced in the extended family. There is nothing strikingly "postmodern" about these families. Stacey herself, struggling for a formula, admits that "the diversity and complexity of postmodern family patterns rivals [sic] that characteristic of premodern kinship forms." But what is gained, then, by calling these patterns "postmodern," "postfeminist," or "postindustrial"? The last of these labels might at least have the merit of calling attention to the deindustrialization of America (as it is more fittingly referred to), which can be expected to add to the economic difficulties that force people to turn to extended families for mutual aid; but the others have no merit of any kind, as far as I can see.

Stacey's data show that working-class women, as always, have trouble holding their families together in times of economic hardship; that they have to contribute to the family's support and even, at times, to assume the full burden of that support; that their experiences with men are not likely to foster romantic illusions about the opposite sex; that they often express damning views of patriarchy which would be the envy of upper-middle-class feminists; that they find it difficult to assume the role of wifely submission (even though many of them covet that role); that they often seek emotional and material support from friends and relatives instead of expecting the nuclear family to provide for all their needs; and that they also seek such support, above all, in religion.

Only an ideology resistant to the unwelcome challenge

of experience can find "democratic opportunity" in this unre-
lenting record of downward mobility, economic and emotional devastation, and domestic improvisation. On the most
favorable reading of the evidence, it establishes the continuing importance of long-term, unconditional commitments—
to God, to husbands or wives—in the efforts of hard-pressed
people to assume responsibility for their lives. The same evidence reminds us, however—on a more unfavorable reading—that such commitments are harder than ever to sustain
in a world full of economic uncertainty, drugs, and cynicism.
The one reading the evidence cannot possibly support is that
working-class women are pioneers of the "postmodern"
family.

The ideology that sustains this bizarre "finding" rests on
three assumptions. The first is that industrialism isolated the
family from the world of work and forced women into the
confining role of full-time housewives. This familiar view of
the family's history underestimates the degree to which even
middle-class women led active lives outside the family, long
after the advent of industrialism, as volunteers in charitable,
philanthropic, and religious organizations—in the case of
working-class women, as wage-earners as well. It also underestimates the family's historic dependence on supporting
networks of relatives, friends, and neighbors. The "isolated
nuclear family" is a sociological abstraction that never had
much empirical substance until the mass migration to the
suburbs, after World War II, broke up the old support systems and made it possible for women to devote themselves,
for a time, exclusively to domesticity. Working-class women,
as Stacey herself recognizes, attained "this long-denied status" just as it was becoming unfashionable, and economic
pressures, in any case, soon forced them back into the labor
force. According to recent polls, most of them would prefer

to stay at home; and it is questionable, therefore, whether the circumstances that oblige them to work for wages are experienced as liberating in their effects. Wage labor is hardly a recent innovation for working-class women, nor does it provide the only escape from full-time domesticity.

A second assumption, that feminism is the only source of self-respect in women, flows from the first. If the cult of domesticity required women to be clinging and submissive, the feminist movement that began in the sixties has finally taught women, presumably, to be strong and self-reliant. Quite apart from the difficulty that feminism itself has a long history, it is clearly absurd to suppose that earlier generations of women, because they did not have access to current insights into the "social construction of gender," deferred mindlessly to men or wore helplessness as a badge of honor. This libel on our mothers and grandmothers seems to derive largely from the media, which have given currency to an abstract image of the "traditional" family that finds little support in the historical record. Stacey notes that "the world's first generation of childhood television-viewers grew up, as I did, inundated by such weekly paeans to the male breadwinner nuclear household and modern family ideology as 'Father Knows Best,' 'Leave It to Beaver,' and 'Ozzie and Harriet.' " No doubt such programs helped to generate a certain "nostalgia" for a type of family life that never existed, as Stacey argues; but they also generated an equally ahistorical contempt for the benighted women in past times who could not grasp the essence of patriarchal oppression, alas, because they had no exposure to "gender studies."

Because Stacey assumes that profamily values are antifeminist by definition, she is repeatedly surprised to find evangelical Christians insisting, for example, that men and women are "equal with God" or that the husband's "headship" of the family does not entitle him to "rule over" his wife, as one of them puts it, but rather to "serve [her] with love and respect." Whenever Stacey encounters such opinions, she describes them as "surprisingly feminized, even protofeminist, doctrines." But "doctrines" have nothing to do with it. One does not have to be a feminist in order to admire strong women, to see through male pretensions of superiority, or to assume responsibility for one's own life.

One of the women interviewed by Stacey, citing pride in her mother as an important influence on her own desire for independence, says: "I don't really know what a feminist is, but I like to take charge of my life, try to be the best in whatever I'm doing. I don't know if that's a feminist or what." Stacey is sure that it is and is therefore puzzled to find that working-class "feminism" can coexist with a belief in the importance of "absolute commitment in marriage," in the words of another informant. For Stacey, such commitments can only be described as a "retreat" from the "arena of postmodern gender and family reform."

Religion, likewise, looks like a "retreat from rationalism and secularism," from Stacey's point of view. The third assumption that dominates and distorts her thinking is that religion interferes with a proper understanding of the world and perpetuates old patterns of domination and dependence. She quotes from her field notes: "I can understand the appeal of such beliefs, but I really can't comprehend how people actually believe this stuff. And on some deep level it depresses and disturbs me that they do." This at least has the virtue of honesty, but it shows a limited understanding even of the "appeal" of religion—its "seductive power," as she puts it elsewhere.

Religion is not just a refuge, a means of security in a troubled world. It is also a challenge to self-pity and despair—

temptations common to all of us, but especially to those born into the wrong social class. Victims of social injustice find it easy to blame everything on systematic oppression—capitalism, patriarchy, racism, the "system" in general. There is value in this way of thinking, if it encourages cooperative resistance to exploitation; but it is also debilitating insofar as it serves merely as an excuse for disclaiming any responsibility for oneself.

Submission to God makes people less submissive in everyday life. It makes them less fearful but also less bitter and resentful, less inclined to make excuses for themselves. Modern social movements, on the other hand, tend to prey on resentment. They aim to make victims acutely aware of their victimization. They distrust any understanding that would seem to "blame the victim." In this way they discourage the assumption of personal responsibility; and then their adherents are "disturbed" and "depressed" when people turn to religion instead!

9

Life in the Therapeutic State

I

The growth of the inward-turning, child-centered family, sociologists have long told us, is one of the distinguishing features of the transition from "traditional" to modern society. In the last twenty years, this theme has been elaborated with an increasing abundance of documentation by social historians—Philippe Ariès, Eli Zaretsky, Edward Shorter, Lawrence Stone, Nancy Cott, and now Carl Degler, to name only those who have attempted large syntheses.

With minor variations from one country to another, the

development of the family has followed the same pattern, it appears, throughout the Western world. By the nineteenth century, young people had won the right to marry with a minimum of direct parental interference. Marriage became a union of individuals rather than a union of two lineages. Companionship rather than parental convenience became the goal of matrimony. A new insistence on the innocence and vulnerability of childhood encouraged a growing preoccupation with child-rearing and especially with maternal influence on the child's development.

In order to give each of their children the advantages to which children were now thought to be entitled, parents deliberately restricted the number of their offspring. Large families gave way to the intimate, private, conjugal unit. A cult of domesticity and a strict division of sexual labor—justified by the doctrine of sexual "spheres"—removed women from the world of work but gave them greater control over the family itself. Shorn of its productive functions, the family now specialized in child-rearing and emotional solace, providing a much-needed sanctuary in a world organized around the impersonal principles of the market.[1]

Drawing on letters and diaries, many of them unpublished; on medical writings; and on the work of other historians (notably Nancy Cott, Linda Gordon, and James C. Mohr), Carl Degler, in his study of the American family *At Odds: Women and the Family in America from the Revolution to the Present* (1980), has filled in this conventional picture, modified some of its details, but left its general outlines untouched. His principal contributions, aside from the sheer weight of evidence he has assembled and his even-tempered treatment of issues that too often serve as incitements to riot, come down to three lines of argument. He has successfully challenged the older view that the Victorians surrounded sex with a "conspiracy of silence." He has shown that Victorian sexual morality, and indeed the whole ideology of domesticity with which it was bound up, was at least in part the creation of women, not a brutal patriarchal ideology designed to keep women in their place. And by demonstrating that women took an active part in the transformation of family life, he has made it more difficult than before to think of the family merely as an institution that responds to impersonal socioeconomic "forces."

The first of these contentions—that the Victorians discussed sex more openly than we have imagined and even took some pleasure in it—has already received a good deal of advance attention. Degler does not argue that the Victorians lived in a sexually permissive paradise, but he denies that they had no understanding of female sexuality. Statements that have been misinterpreted as evidence that Victorian physicians denied the existence of sexual appetites in women should be read instead as prescriptive statements, designed to support a new morality to the effect that a male should not "obtrude himself upon the unwilling female," as one medical authority put it. Since men had no particular interests of their own in restricting sexual activity, Degler reasons, sexual restraint must be seen not as a morality imposed on women but as part of their attempt to free themselves from repeated pregnancies.

This argument is closely related to a second line of reasoning. The cult of domesticity, in this view, was no more a limitation imposed on women than a restrictive sexual morality was. Nineteenth-century domesticity rested on the principle of companionship, and women appealed to this principle, according to Degler, in order to justify not only their right to protect themselves but many other demands. The cult of domesticity, though it confined women to the home, made them the moral arbiters of the family and of whatever else touched its interests.

By exploiting this ideology, women won greater autonomy in marriage and launched social campaigns to abolish prostitution (or at least to withdraw social sanction from it), to raise the age of consent, to control the intake of alcoholic beverages, and otherwise to protect women from male violence and sexual harassment. "One of the arguments of this book," Degler writes, "is that the history of the family is best understood by recognizing that changes in the role of women have been at the root of that history." This rather bland formulation conceals the more interesting thesis that women actively reshaped the family in pursuit of their own interests, turning the cult of domesticity against itself and thereby laying the basis of modern feminism. Demands for the recognition of married women's property rights, for divorce laws favoring the wife, for sexual self-control on the part of men, for acknowledgment of the woman's greater stake in regulating the frequency of sexual intercourse and pregnancy, and even for larger reforms in the field of social justice and "social purity"—all arose out of the logic of domesticity itself and succeeded, according to Degler, for that very reason.

That feminism took support from the very ideology it seemed to challenge—the cult of domesticity—will come as no surprise to careful students of nineteenth-century history, certainly not to readers of the work of Aileen Kraditor and Nancy Cott.[2] The implications of this development remain to be explored, however, and Degler's book, merely because it is the first to deal with domesticity and feminism in the same place, at first sight promises to advance our understanding of their dialectical interplay. Unfortunately his treatment of feminism, and even to some extent of domesticity itself, bogs down in confusion and contradictions.

At Odds is not a closely argued book. Degler hedges, for example, on the important question of whether women managed to restrict the frequency of sexual intercourse in opposition to their husbands, or whether men cooperated because they took the idea of companionship seriously and also perhaps had economic reasons, after all, for wishing to limit the size of their families. Did the practice of sexual restraint, reflected in declining fertility, reflect a "close and communicative relationship between husband and wife" or a breakdown of communication? Did nineteenth-century middle-class marriage encourage "mutual consideration" or conflict?

Although conflict certainly seems to be implied by Degler's central thesis that women were "at odds" with the family, most of the time he prefers to stress "closeness and mutual influence between husband and wife." If cooperation was the rule, however, it becomes difficult to explain why nineteenth-century women (feminists and antifeminists alike) so often regarded men as antagonists and preferred the company of their own sex.[3]

Degler waffles, then, on the question of whether declining birth rates reflected women's victory over their husbands or, on the other hand, a victory for companionship and "close communication." But his argument on this point is a model of consistency compared to his analysis of feminism. On the one hand, Degler maintains that the feminist demand for the vote, alone among the various reforms advanced by nineteenth-century women, challenged the doctrine of sexual "spheres." Feminists "made no attempt to conceal the conflict between feminism and the traditional family." Unfortunately most of their sisters were not yet ready to "alter the traditional family and woman's role in it," and their opposition (much more than the opposition of men) postponed the adoption of woman suffrage for many decades.

On the other hand, Degler argues a few pages later that woman suffrage "did not disrupt the family" at all and that antifeminist fears were therefore misguided. Indeed he thinks it is too bad that feminists didn't "confront" the family more directly. They wanted women to take part as equals in the world of politics and work but refused to admit that such a program conflicted with the "traditional" family structure that required women to be full-time wives and mothers. Instead of facing up to this contradiction, feminists backed down from their initial assertion that votes for women "symbolized their individuality [and] their need to speak politically as individuals," and rested the case for suffrage on the more conservative grounds that women as moral custodians "had a special contribution to make to society." If women were given the vote, feminists now claimed, they would abolish the traffic in liquor and women, put an end to political corruption, and advance the work of "social housekeeping."

Some of these assertions are refuted by Degler's own evidence. Having shown that large numbers of middle-class women—women who did not regard themselves as feminists at all—had "challenged the family" on many issues, from the 1830s on, he cannot very well argue that these same women opposed woman suffrage because it challenged the "traditional" family. It seems more reasonable to assume—in the absence of a thorough study of the opposition to woman's suffrage, which has yet to be made—that most women correctly perceived that voting would do little to advance their immediate interests, either as women struggling against the remnants of patriarchal authority or, in the case of lower-class women, as members of an exploited social class. Working-class women wanted not the abstract recognition of equal rights but special protection for women in factories. Women who lived on farms, at a time when the conditions of agrarian life were deteriorating at a fearful rate, had more important things to worry about than the suffrage. It is significant that the Populist party, which included a considerable number of politically active women, refused to endorse woman suffrage in 1892—not because it shows that even radical women held conservative opinions on the family, as Degler reasons, but because radical women presumably recognized that feminism, a middle-class movement addressed to the middle-class woman's need for self-expression, had little to offer women who faced the more immediate threat of poverty.

If the feminist movement posed no threat to the socioeconomic status quo, however, this was not because feminists failed to "challenge" the family. On this point Degler relies on earlier interpretations of nineteenth-century feminism—those of Aileen Kraditor and William O'Neill—that are about to be drastically revised in a forthcoming study by William R. Leach.[4] Kraditor and O'Neill maintain that suffragists gave up arguments based on justice and embraced the conservative position that suffrage would extend women's purifying influence over all of public life. Leach shows, on the contrary, that feminists saw the reform of marriage as the central issue and advocated suffrage as one method of equalizing the relations between men and women. Far from denying that suffrage would "force an alteration in the traditional family," feminists advocated it precisely for that reason. Yet their vision of an egalitarian family based on the economic independence of women remained, for all its radicalism, a class program, closely tied to the outlook and interests of an emerging professional class seeking new forms of control over the sexual and social conflicts which threatened, in their eyes, to tear American society to pieces.

It is my own contention that American progressivism— of which the feminist movement constituted an integral part—has to be seen, as Charles A. Beard proposed at the time, as a "counter-reformation." Progressivism represented a highly successful attempt to deflect Populism, labor radicalism, and other potentially revolutionary movements by reforming society from the top down. Feminists, like other progressives, advocated not individualism but social "cooperation," starting with marriage. They sought to control sexuality, greed, aggression, and other socially disruptive passions by diverting them into harmless outlets. William James's famous essay on the "moral equivalent of war" is an example of a type of thinking that runs through progressivism and through feminism as well. Feminists assumed, moreover, that women, more cooperatively disposed than men and less heavily committed to the masculine pursuits of war and competitive profit-seeking, could change society by infiltrating the major institutions (government, business, education, the service professions) and turning them to more peaceful purposes. The "expediency" argument for woman suffrage has to be seen as a particular application of the general progressive principle that the "best" people should govern—people qualified, that is, by allegedly disinterested motives and plenty of professional training.

Like other progressives, nineteenth-century feminists had a boundless faith in disinterested scientific expertise. They proposed to organize both sexual life and social life according to the principles of modern science, and they had nothing but contempt for those (like the Populists) who tried to base political action on the native intelligence of ordinary men and women. It is not surprising, under these conditions, that ordinary men and women did not rush to support woman suffrage.

It is impossible to make sense of the history of the nineteenth-century family—as the inconsistencies and contradictions in Degler's argument suggest—unless we see the drive to "control sexuality," as he puts it, as part of a larger campaign to control everything else as well—to put society under the microscope. The emotional intensification of family life—the new "intimacy" on which Degler and others have lavished so much admiring attention—led not to cooperation but to conflicts between husbands and wives and between parents and children. These conflicts laid bare the sexual attraction between parents and children and the complications to which it later gives rise in the relations between adult men and women. Nineteenth-century "alienists" and health reformers already understood the connection between sexual repression and neurosis, and, as Degler shows, they also knew a good deal about infantile sexuality. To enlightened members of the professional classes—and this includes most feminists—knowledge of this kind promised a preventive science of sexual and social control, which could be used among other things to civilize the poor, to subject them to new controls sincerely disguised as benevolence, and thus to integrate them more fully into the emerging industrial order.

Because Degler adopts the conventional distinction between "social feminism" and the suffrage movement, he cannot see that efforts to control sexuality in the family were inspired by the same drive that found expression in progressivism—the drive to bring dangerous energies, social or sexual, under control. The achievement of "individualism" and "autonomy" for middle-class women represented part of a larger social and political process that ended in the ascendancy of professional experts.

Degler misses one of the most striking features of the late nineteenth-century American scene—the alliance between women and doctors and the irony of its result. Because professional intervention in family life eroded patriarchal

authority, women sought professional help—or at least welcomed it when it was offered—even when it also eroded the
traditional prerogatives of women. Thus women welcomed
the substitution of doctors for midwives in childbirth. The
redefinition of pregnancy as a disease requiring medical intervention helped women in their campaign for voluntary
motherhood by raising the cost of pregnancy to their husbands—not only the financial cost but the emotional cost of
the doctor's intrusion into the bedroom, his usurpation of
the husband's sexual prerogatives. In the long run, however,
professionals expanded their jurisdiction over domestic life
not only at the expense of patriarchal authority but also at
the expense of the authority formerly exercised by women
over childbirth, child-rearing, and domestic economy. Doctors, psychiatrists, social workers, child guidance experts, and
other specialists derided maternal instinct, home remedies,
and rule-of-thumb methods, claiming to substitute for the
traditional lore of women new techniques based on science
and understood only by those with professional training. In
allying themselves with the helping professions, women
improved their position in the family only to fall into a new
kind of dependence, the dependence of the consumer on the
market and on the providers of expert services, not only for
the satisfaction of their needs but for the very definition of
their needs.

II

For a better understanding of these issues, we have to
turn to the studies by Michel Foucault and Jacques Donzelot.
Like so many French intellectuals, these writers take no
account of historical developments outside France and show
no acquaintance with English or American scholarship. Nev-

ertheless their studies cover some of the same ground discussed by Degler. Foucault's *History of Sexuality: Volume I, An Introduction* (1978), like Degler's book, takes issue with the received wisdom that the nineteenth century surrounded sex with a conspiracy of silence. But Foucault does not make the mistake of assuming that nineteenth-century attitudes were therefore more enlightened than we have assumed, or that they foreshadow the sexual liberation of our own time— for which he holds no brief in any case. He challenges not only the conventional picture of nineteenth-century sexual repression but the ideology of sexual emancipation itself. "We must not think that by saying yes to sex, one says no to power."

The achievement of sexual freedom, in Foucault's view, has to be seen as another aspect of the medicalization of life, resulting not in a richer emotional experience but in a more thoroughgoing surveillance and control of sexuality. The extension of medical jurisdiction over sex, replacing the ecclesiastical jurisdiction of the old regime, belongs historically to the growth of the disciplinary apparatus analyzed in Foucault's earlier works—*Madness and Civilization, The Birth of the Clinic,* and *Discipline and Punish.* In those studies, he argued that the reform of criminal justice, the "moral treatment" of the insane, and the abandonment of public torture cannot be attributed merely to the influence of nineteenth-century humanitarianism. Nineteenth-century philanthropists, whatever their intentions, created a more effective and pervasive system of social control based on systematic observation and surveillance. Similarly the exposure of sexual life to scientific scrutiny contributed to the rationalization, not the liberation, of emotional life.

Volubility, not silence, characterized the nineteenth-century approach to sex, according to Foucault: the translation of emotion into discourse. Far from suppressing an awareness of sexual appetites, the medical profession encouraged people to speak of them fully and with an abundance of detail. "An immense verbosity is what our civilization has required and organized." The details of sexual activity came to be valued for the symptomatic insights they provided into the formation of personality, child-rearing, family life, and into broader problems of social hygiene.

Medicine now upheld what American observers have called a normative schedule of psychosocial development, deviations from which doctors attempt to correct (not to punish) by means of appropriate pedagogical and philanthropic measures. In place of moral norms, the new style of social discipline substituted a set of medical and psychological norms from which moral questions, questions of commendation and censure, were rigorously excluded. Doctors, criminologists, alienists, and other members of the learned professions—to which in the twentieth century were added social workers, psychiatrists, educators, marriage counselors, child development experts, pediatricians, parole officers, judges of the juvenile courts, in short the modern apparatus of resocialization—governed society not "by right but by technique, not by law but by normalization, not by punishment but by control." Foucault describes the origins and dynamics of what others (Philip Rieff, Nicholas Kittrie) have called the therapeutic state.

In order to identify the characteristic features of the modern attitude toward sex, and to distinguish it from earlier traditions, Foucault compares the scientific attitude to the classical and Oriental "art of love," which organized sexual experience as a body of closely guarded secrets transmitted—like other sacred mysteries—from master to disciple. The master initiated the novice into esoteric information and guided his progress "with unfailing skill and severity."

The Counter-Reformation confessional, according to Foucault, represented the first break with the ancient art of love. Just as Ariès saw in the Counter-Reformation a new concern with the formation of personality and the discipline of childhood (and with discipline in general), and Foucault himself in his earlier work saw the "great confinement" of the seventeenth century as the beginning of a concerted attempt to subject poverty, crime, and insanity to the organized discipline of the state—the "new medicine for poverty," as R. H. Tawney called it—so Foucault now finds another expression of this social impulse in the reform of the Catholic ritual of confession. "Beginning in the sixteenth century, this rite gradually detached itself from the sacrament of penance, and via the guidance of souls and the direction of conscience . . . emigrated toward pedagogy, relationships between adults and children, family relations, medicine, and psychiatry." The Christian tradition of penitential self-examination became the basis of the modern *scientia sexualis*, which adapted the "ancient procedure of confession to the rules of scientific discourse." In the nineteenth century, "the same doctors who sought to control disease by subjecting it to medical scrutiny hoped to manage and administer sexual activity by means of analytical discourses." The psychoanalytic confession represented a later elaboration of the same procedures.

The growing medical recognition of the importance of sex in personality formation gave doctors a new stake in the supervision of child-rearing and family life. The nineteenth-century family became the chief agency for what Foucault calls the deployment of sexuality. By subjecting the sexual pathology of the family to closer investigation, doctors tried to stem the rising tide of "modern nervousness," perversion, masturbation, prostitution, venereal disease, physical and moral degeneracy. The family itself, encouraged by experts, "engaged in searching out the slightest traces of sexuality in its midst, wrenching from itself the most difficult confessions, soliciting an audience with everyone who might know something about the matter, and opening itself unreservedly to endless examination."

Perhaps because *The History of Sexuality* was intended as the first of several volumes on the subject, Foucault does not elaborate on the subject of the family. But his follower and colleague Jacques Donzelot has extended Foucault's analysis of modern discipline in *The Policing of Families* (1979). The freshness of Donzelot's analysis is striking when it is compared to Degler's more conventional treatment of somewhat similar issues. Donzelot, like Degler, understands the connections between the nineteenth-century cult of domesticity, as it has come to be called by American scholars, and the emancipation of women. He sees that "birth control and the 'liberation' of women rested on women's old social vocation, on their function of ambassadresses of culture."

But he also sees what eludes Degler: that women's role as cultural missionaries, closely bound up with their domestic confinement but simultaneously serving to justify demands for wider social influence and participation in public life, was to some extent the deliberate creation of doctors seeking to make wives and mothers agents of medical influence—of the medical "colonization" of the family. Foucault, as we have seen, rejects the commonsensical interpretation of nineteenth-century moral progress, according to which the rise of humanitarianism led to the decline of public torture. A similar interpretation of family history has been offered by historians like Edward Shorter, Lawrence Stone, and Degler, who

see the growth of intimacy, the rise of "companionate marriage," a more enlightened attitude toward sex, and a new
respect for children as the principal ingredients in nineteenth-century domesticity.

Although Donzelot does not confront this interpretation
directly, his book implicitly repudiates it, on the same
grounds that led Foucault to reject another version of the
Whiggish interpretation of the past. The "privatization" of
middle-class family life, described by Ariès and by English
and American historians who have followed his lead,
occurred at the same time that other influences were opening
the family to medical surveillance and control. Donzelot's
is one of the first studies to do justice to both sides of this
development—the new value set on privacy, on the one
hand, and the invasion of privacy, on the other hand, by the
"tutelary apparatus" of the modern state.[5]

The conventional interpretation of the family's history, as
it has emerged in the last twenty years, not only misses the
ironic outcome of well-intentioned reforms (the rationalization of private life) but also ignores the antagonistic social
relations in which these reforms took shape. The bourgeois
cult of domesticity defined itself in opposition to aristocratic
license on the one hand and to popular immorality on the
other. Under the old regime, the state rested on the family,
or more accurately on the system of matrimonial alliances
that controlled the succession of property. Nineteenth-century philanthropists objected to the old arrangements on the
grounds that matrimonial choices ought to be determined by
eugenic rather than economic considerations. They claimed
that the old-fashioned education of women, instead of training them for motherhood, trained them only in the arts of
sexual attraction. In their eyes the old system of arranged
marriage, by treating women solely as ornaments, objects of

matrimonial exchange, encouraged habits of dissipation in both sexes. It perpetuated the notorious double standard of sexual morality, hypocritically condemning the sexual irregularities it encouraged in women while condoning them in men. It gave rise to prostitution and venereal diseases, which were sapping the nation's health. In short, the system of matrimonial exchange corrupted sex and marriage by subordinating them to the advancement of private ends—the family's economic and dynastic ambitions.

Because the philanthropic critique of conventional marriage turned on the same issues raised by advocates of romantic love, spokesmen for the rights of children, educational reformers, and feminists, it is easy to miss the hygienic intentions behind the reform of marriage or the extension of medical authority over family life. Doctors sided with the weaker members of the family against patriarchal authority. They sought to make women agents of a new medical morality. In the "privileged alliance between doctor and mother," however, the mother remained a subordinate partner. As Donzelot (or rather his translator) puts it, "The doctor prescribes, the mother executes."

Accordingly the family emerged at the end of the nineteenth century as a "hothouse insulated against outside influences" but subject, at the same time, to close medical surveillance. Children achieved independence from parental control but fell increasingly under the control of the state. "Family patriarchalism was destroyed only at the cost of a patriarchy of the state."

Donzelot shows that the destruction of the alliance system went hand in hand with the domestication of the poor, as it might be called. At the beginning of the nineteenth century, doctors and civil servants began to argue that irregular unions among the poor, illegitimacy, incest, and other forms of sexual immorality kept the lower orders in a state of chronic demoralization, prevented them from becoming industrious workers, and made them dependent on public charity. By encouraging orderly habits of domesticity, reformers hoped to make them sober and self-supporting. Here again, they tried to play off the housewife against her husband and to make women the arbiters of domestic morality. In Donzelot's formulation, they replaced a government of families with a government through the family.

These reforms eroded "popular enclaves that allowed for autonomous ties between the generations." Relations between parents and children came under the supervision of the state, as executed by the schools, the social work agencies, and the juvenile court. The supervisory apparatus, Donzelot points out, "fostered mistrust among [the family's] members" while eradicating the adversary relation between the child and the court, thereby creating a situation in which the rights of the family depended on its willingness to cooperate with the machinery of law enforcement. The juvenile court replaced punishment with prevention, judgment with surveillance. It treated the adolescent's offenses as symptoms of an unhealthy domestic environment, which justified the "technicians of human relations" in launching inquiries into family morality, removing the child from his home if necessary, and demanding that families comply with the new principles of social hygiene.

Parents who called in the police or social workers, in the hope that outside intervention would strengthen their authority over a wayward child, found instead that it transferred the child to a professional authority. "Instead of the desired admonition, the juvenile judge, after reviewing the results of the social inquiry [the social worker's case report], decides in favor of an educative assistance that has another purpose altogether, since it brings the adolescent into the sphere of the tutelary complex, leading to his detachment from family authority and transferral to a social authority, . . . all in order to prevent him from contaminating his brothers and sisters and to enable his parents to devote themselves to the younger children."

Naturally the architects of the juvenile court justified their activities on humanitarian grounds. They argued that it would make the court a friend of the juvenile offender and an ally of the family. "But these are pious representations," according to Donzelot, "of reasons that are much less 'democratic.' " Philanthropic intervention in the family, he argues, was a "deliberately depoliticizing strategy." Inspired by a fear of class conflict, it belonged to a general attempt to control the poor, to counter socialist propaganda, and to transform political procedures into administrative procedures. Reformers designed a new style of domestic life as an alternative both to the paternalism of the old regime, which made the lower classes dependent on charity and *noblesse oblige*, and to socialism. In their calculations, hygienic and political considerations were "indissociable."

Only if we see the modern "companionate" family as a liberal solution to the problems of industrial society, according to Donzelot—in particular, to the problem of countering industrial unrest without creating an all-powerful authoritarian state—can we understand its distinctive characteristics. Liberals in France (and in other countries as well) tried to steer between conservative paternalists, who upheld the family as the basis of the social order and saw every change as a threat to the integrity of the domestic unit, and socialists, who wanted to replace parenthood with the state. In the end they outflanked their adversaries by creating a therapeutic state which left the family more or less intact yet subjected it to nonstop supervision.

The new machinery of therapeutic intervention mediated between "familialist" and socialist strategies and eventually rendered both of them obsolete. The polemics that swirled around the family in the early twentieth century now have an archaic flavor (in spite of their revival in the 1970s). We can no longer take very seriously either the outcry about race suicide and the imminent extinction of family life or, on the other hand, the socialist-medical utopia that envisioned total state control over reproduction. The modern family in the West is neither patriarchal nor socialist. It is an "advanced liberal family," in Donzelot's words, attended by a "little army of counselors and psychologists" who neither "assign anyone, dictatorially, to family life" nor "aim to destroy family life."

The triumph of the therapeutic, as Philip Rieff called it, has provided the liberal state with a new system of indirect controls that preserves the appearance and even some of the reality of private initiative—in the family as in the economy—within a larger structure of professional supervision. In this sense Freud proved to be the Keynes of the family, according to Donzelot. What Donzelot describes as the psychoanalytic point of view—but is better described as a "relational fever" common to both behavioral and humanistic psychology, and having little to do with psychoanalysis as such—provides a new morality that blames "nothing in particular and everything in general." The therapeutic apparatus subjects the family to "social management" as opposed to the direct intervention of the state. It saves the "familial reference without which 'possessive individualism' has no functional possibilities" yet keeps a watchful eye on the pathology of the nuclear family, seeking to free individuals from its excessive emotional demands. In short, it leaves the family "always 'justified' in theory and always suspect in practice."

Much of the current public debate about the family, in the United States and no doubt in France as well, continues to be informed by outmoded assumptions. Ever since the Fifties, the left has periodically deplored the revival of pro-family sentiment, as if the modern cult of the "companionate," "developmental," and psychiatric family signaled a revival of patriarchal authority in all its severity.[6] The right, on the other hand, sees in the extension of therapeutic controls the menace of statism (among other things). Efforts to understand how these controls work, to describe their effects on marriage and on the socialization of the young, are immediately absorbed into an older, obsolete debate about the "future of the family." The right applauds such investigations as an ideological defense of the family, the left condemns them as a plea for the revival of patriarchal authority, and the social service professions seek to incorporate them into their own never-ending campaign for a more effective "policy on families."

Thus Carl Degler's book ends—just as one would expect it to end—with a discussion of the false and meaningless issue of whether the family has a future. The continuing popularity of this empty debate offers another example of the way in which attention has been displaced onto "the family" that would better be paid to the changing quality of the relations between men and women, parents and children. Degler mounts the familiar argument that the high rate of remarriage, the lengthening of the time children stay at home, and the lack of any increase in the number of women electing to remain childless all indicate—notwithstanding a declining birth rate and a rising divorce rate—that the family is "here to stay."[7]

But this argument about the survival of the family is beside the point. The conventional understanding of family history generates such a debate only because it treats the "crisis of the family," as Donzelot points out, "as the result of an evolution of mores, the development of psychologism and psychoanalysm as the solution." A more penetrating view, one that stresses the "genealogy of counseling," as Donzelot calls it, gives no support either to the right or left, much less to the psychiatric apparatus which seeks to mediate between them (and which, as he observes, is equally compatible with an ideological defense of the family and a Laingian indictment of the family). Such an interpretation traces the collapse of patriarchal authority and the rise of therapeutic authority, and thus makes it equally pointless to call for the revival of patriarchy and to condemn the modern family as an agency of continuing patriarchal domination.

This new interpretation of the family's history also undermines the position of those who call so urgently for solutions to the "crisis of the family." Donzelot resolutely refuses to offer any constructive proposals for change. To offer them, he insists, is to accept the historical assumptions on which the demand for practical solutions rests. What becomes of this demand, he asks,

> When we challenge its assumptions, when we identify the emergence of the modern family and the expansion of "psy" organizations as a single process, and one that is not politically innocent in the least? . . . Instead of being lured into the search for a solution to the obvious malaises that develop around and within family life, we shall ask ourselves: This crisis of the family, *together with* this proliferation of "psy" activities, are themselves the solution to what problem?

The answer to this question should now be clear. The problem—the solution to which occupied much of the social imagination of the last two centuries—was to replace a discredited patriarchal authority with a new form of social discipline that stops short of total domination by the state. But this new style of noncoercive, nonauthoritative, and manipulative control poses its own kind of danger to the democratic institutions it is intended to preserve. Here my own perception of the current situation may begin to diverge from Donzelot's. He sees Freud and Keynes as the two great stabilizers of the liberal order. Leaving aside his too close identification of Freud with a "tutelary apparatus" that owes more to his detractors and revisionists, I think Donzelot overlooks the instability of both the Keynesian and the psychiatric modes of adjustment.

Keynesian economics helped to control some of the chronic problems of liberal capitalism but provided no long-term solution, as we can now see all too clearly. The same thing can be said of therapeutic modes of social control. These controls create new forms of dependence and discourage participation in political life. In so doing they simplify some of the problems of social discipline but at the same time make it more and more difficult for political leaders to mobilize public support of their policies when the need arises. Voter "apathy," popular indifference and cynicism, the national "malaise" to which our leaders direct our attention all testify to the erosion of older mechanisms of popular participation and the reduction of the citizen to a consumer of expertise.

A passive, suspicious, apolitical electorate can no longer be roused by appeals for national solidarity. Leaders who preach sacrifice to such an electorate are wasting their breath. In a society that remains formally democratic, people will make sacrifices only in support of policies they have had a hand in drawing up. The new mechanisms of therapeutic control, however, tend to exclude people from active participation in political life or in any of the other decisions that affect them. The directors of the therapeutic state, having to some extent pacified a formerly rebellious population, now find themselves confronted by a full-scale "crisis of confidence."

In the 1980 primary election in New York, a Manhattan housewife explained that she intended to vote for Kennedy, reluctantly, because she was tired of hearing from President Carter about the sacrifices he expects her to make in the austere times ahead. "I hate Carter," she said. "Carter tells me I'm going to suffer. I don't want to suffer." This statement dramatizes the "crisis of confidence" that faces liberal leaders.

The prospects for the liberal state, in its therapeutic as in its Keynesian manifestation, are not good. In the days ahead, it will either have to adopt openly dictatorial forms of control or give way to a more truly democratic system. In the meantime, those who care about the "future of the family" would do well to follow Donzelot's lead and to have nothing to do with the official search for a national policy on families. What the family needs is a policy on officials, designed to keep them in their place.

NOTES

1. The following observations by the psychologist Jerome Kagan, approvingly cited by Degler in support of his prediction of the "continuance of the family," provide a representative specimen of conventional thinking on this subject: "As modern environments make a sense of potency and individual effectiveness more difficult to attain, freedom from all affective involvements becomes more and more intolerable. Involvement with a family is the only viable mechanism available to satisfy that hunger." In other words, the family, according to the conven-

tional sociological wisdom, has come to serve as a "haven in a heartless world."

2. Aileen S. Kraditor, *The Ideas of the Woman Suffrage Movement* (Columbia University Press, 1965); Nancy F. Cott, *The Bonds of Womanhood* (Yale University Press, 1977). Degler's book draws heavily on both these interpretations.

3. Probably the root of this difficulty lies in the idea that women were "at odds" with a sociological abstraction of more interest to scholars and to professional helpers than to ordinary men and women—"the family." In fact they were more often at odds with men. Not only scholars but feminists (surprisingly) shy away from this fact, however. In spite of all the recent talk about women's interests, women's rights, and women's struggle to achieve full citizenship, the assertion that men and women are seriously and in some ways fundamentally "at odds" still strikes most progressive-minded people not only as an erroneous but—more reprehensibly, from their point of view—as a reactionary interpretation of the matter. Everybody agrees that "the family" oppresses women, but nobody is in any hurry to take a serious look at the oppression of women by men. I think I know the reason for this reluctance: such an investigation might lead to the conclusion, abhorrent to the sensibility of our enlightened age, that not every conflict has an obvious institutional resolution. This squeamishness about sexual conflict explains why feminists, social workers, sociologists, and other professional critics of domestic arrangements confine their attacks to "the family"—a safe target, since "the family" can't fight back, and men these days, moreover, have their own reasons (as always) to reject the values associated with domestic life.

4. O'Neill's *Everyone Was Brave: The Rise and Fall of Feminism in America* was published by Quadrangle in 1969. Leach's study, *True Love and Perfect Union: The Feminist Reform of Sex and Society*, was published in 1980 by Basic Books.

5. Richard Sennett, in a review of *The Policing of Families* (*The New York Times Book Review*, February 24, 1980), claims to find a "divergence" between Donzelot's interpretation of family history and the one I presented in *Haven in a Heartless World*. "For Mr. Lasch, the history of the modern bourgeois family is a history of the state 'invading' the functions of the family through welfare bureaucracies, psychiatric controls, and other professional organs. For Mr. Donzelot, the invasion image is wrong. From the middle of the eighteenth century, he contends, the state has actively participated in creating the forms of family life that we know today."

I have no idea what this last sentence is supposed to mean. What concerns me, however, is that readers of Sennett's review will get the impression that Donzelot explicitly repudiates the imagery of invasion and refrains from using such imagery himself. In fact, he speaks repeatedly of the "colonization" of the family by the helping professions, of their "full penetration" of the family, of their "ceaseless technocratic interventionism," of the "continuous surveillance" they exercise over domestic life, of the "extension of medical control," and of the "transfer of sovereignty" from the family to a corrective system that "never stops swelling." I don't know why Sennett prefers the vague, noncommittal formula of "active participation," but such euphemisms play no part in Donzelot's account.

Like other careless readers, Sennett detects in my own work a "kind of nostalgia for the virtues of the nineteenth-century bourgeois family," whereas Donzelot, he writes, "feels no such regrets." Maybe not; but he describes very clearly, in several passages, the modern definition of liberation as freedom from family ties and the search for low-keyed, undemanding, nonneurotic relationships free of the emotional ambivalence associated with family relationships. The modern therapeutic outlook, he writes, regards emotional "maturation not [as] the acceptance of a heritage, a destiny, but the fading significance of one's family, escape from its desires, liberation from the possessive desires of one's parents." It is the historical accuracy of such statements—and of similar statements in my own work—that is, or ought to be, at issue. I leave to others the weighty question of whether they encourage a politically debilitating "nostalgia" for the old regime.

6. Writers on the left find it almost impossible to introduce an essay on the family without performing this obligatory ritual. "We are witnessing a significant retreat from the experimental mode [of the Sixties]. The nuclear family is back in favor, both within the wider society and within the women's movement. This retreat is being duly registered in the academy" (Wini Breines, Margaret Cerullo, and Judith Stacey, "Social Biology, Family Studies, and Antifeminist Backlash," *Feminist Studies*, February 4, 1978, p. 43). "Patriarchal societies have always associated social disintegration with women's activism. . . . Politically, pro-family and anti-feminist forces emerged from their closets around the issue of the proposed White House Conference on the Family. . . . On both scholarly and popular levels, feminism has generated distress that manifests responses ranging from scorn to 'backlash' " (Sandi E. Cooper, "Feminism and Family Revivalism," *Chrysalis*, summer 1979, pp. 58, 60–61).

Eli Zaretsky opens a recent paper on "The Welfare State and the Family" in the same vein: "A striking political development during the past several years has been the emergence of a pro-family consensus among almost every group concerned with the issue. . . . This near unanimous support for the family has the quality of a return of the repressed after a period of challenges to traditional ideals of the family. . . . The call to 'strengthen the family' embodies the conservative mood of the moment."

All these exercises in trend-spotting miss the point. The "call to strengthen the family" comes from the same therapeutic professions that identified themselves, only a few years ago, with the radical critique of the repressive nuclear family. They have no particular stake in the question of whether the "crisis of the family" derives from the persistence of patriarchal oppression of women or from the collapse of patriarchy. Their only stake lies in public acknowledgment of a crisis that can be resolved only by their own intervention. Professional commentators on the family are professional crisis-managers, not ideologues. They can easily adapt themselves to changing political and journalistic fashions.

7. Like Mary Jo Bane (*Here to Stay*, Basic Books, 1976) and many other commentators, Degler claims that divorce is no more disruptive than the early deaths that used to disrupt family life. But the important question is whether children experience these disruptions in the same way—which seems unlikely. Instead of addressing this analytical issue, most commentators take refuge in the normative cliché that "from the standpoint of the children," as Degler puts it, "an end to an unhappy marriage is probably preferable to living in a household characterized by tension and acrimony."

Index